THE OLDEST CUISINE IN THE WORLD

Jean Bottéro

THE OLDEST CUISINE IN THE WORLD

Cooking in Mesopotamia

TRANSLATED BY TERESA LAVENDER FAGAN

THE UNIVERSITY OF CHICAGO PRESS
CHICAGO AND LONDON

The University of Chicago Press, Chicago 60637
The University of Chicago Press, Ltd., London
© 2004 by The University of Chicago
All rights reserved. Published 2004
Printed and bound by CPI Group (UK) Ltd, Croydon, CR0 4YY

19 18 17 16 15 14 13 12 11   2 3 4 5 6

ISBN-13: 978-0-226-06735-3 (cloth)
ISBN-13: 978-0-226-06734-6 (paper)
ISBN-10: 0-226-06735-1 (cloth)
ISBN-10: 0-226-06734-3 (paper)

Originally published in Paris as *La plus vieille
cuisine du monde*, © Editions Louis Audibert, 2002.

The University of Chicago Press gratefully acknowledges a subvention from the govern-
ment of France through the French Ministry of Culture, Centre du Livre, in support of
the costs of translating this volume.

Library of Congress Cataloging-in-Publication Data

Bottéro Jean.
   [Plus vieille cuisine du monde. English]
   The oldest cuisine in the world ; cooking in Mesopotamia / Jean Bottéro ;
translated by Teresa Lavender Fagan.
      p.   cm.
   Includes bibliographical references.
   ISBN 0-226-06735-1 (cloth : alk. paper)
   1. Cookery, Iraqi—History.   2. Food habits—Iraq—History.
3. Iraq—Social life and customs.   I. Title.
TX725.I72B68   2004
641.5935—dc22

                                                    2003061292

TO THE FRIENDSHIP AND COMPETENCE OF
LOUIS AUDIBERT,
WITHOUT WHOM THIS BOOK
WOULD NEVER HAVE BEEN POSSIBLE.

CONTENTS

TRANSLATOR'S NOTE

It has been a particularly great pleasure to translate this book on Meso-potamian cuisine, for in the course of my work I thought often of the au-thor, whom I met for the first time at his home outside Paris a few years ago. On that lovely spring afternoon my daughter and I shared a meal with him and his family—a delicious meal he had prepared himself. I then came to know another Jean Bottéro: not the renowned expert on an-cient Mesopotamia, but the gracious host, fine cook, and delightful table companion. I saw firsthand his delight in and respect for *le manger et le boire*—eating and drinking good food and drink in the company of friends and family. That afternoon and the author's warm good cheer have in-spired my work on this translation. I raise a glass—and a fork!—in his honor.

ABBREVIATIONS

AbB:	*Altbabylonische Briefe.*
AbB I:	Kraus, F.R. *Altbabylonische Briefe: Briefe aus dem British Museum* (CT 43 and 44). Leiden, 1964.
AbB II:	Frankena, R. *Altbabylonische Briefe: Briefe aus dem British Museum* (LIH and CT 2–33). Leiden, 1966.
AbB VI	Frankena, R. *Altbabylonische Briefe: Briefe aus dem Berliner Museum.* Leiden, 1974.
AfO	*Archiv für Orientforschung.*
ARM	*Archives royales de Mari.*
ARM VII	Bottéro, J. *Archives royales de Mari: Textes économiques et administratifs.* Paris, 1957.
ARM I	Birot, M. *Archives royales de Mari: Textes administratifs de la salle 5 du Palais.* Paris, 1960.
ARM XI	Burke, M.-L. *Archives royales de Mari: Textes administratifs de la salle 11 du Palais.* Paris, 1963.
ARM XII	Birot, M. *Archives royales de Mari: Textes administratifs de la salle 5 du Palais (2e partie).* Paris, 1964.
ARM XXI	Durand, J.-M. *Archives royales de Mari: Textes administratifs des salles 134 et 160 du Palais de Mari.* Paris, 1983.
BaM	*Baghdader Mitteilungen.*
CAD	*Chicago Assyrian Dictionary,* Chicago, 1956–.
CT	*Cuneiform Texts from Babylonian Tablets in the British Museum,* vols. 1–58. London, 1896–.
DP	Allotte de la Fuÿe, M. *Documents présargoniques.* Paris, 1908–.
HSS	*Harvard Semitic Series.*

HSS XIII	Pfeiffer, R.H., and E.-R. Lacheman. *Excavations at Nuzi IV.* Cambridge, Mass., 1942.
JCS	*Journal of Cuneiform Studies.*
KAR	Ebeling, E. *Keilschrifttexte aus Assur religiösen Inhalts,* Leipzig, 1915–.
MSL V	Landsberger, B. *The Series HAR-ra: hubullu, Tablets I–V.* Rome, 1957.
MSL VIII/2	Landsberger, B. *The Fauna of Ancient Mesopotamia II.* Rome, 1962.
MSL XI	Landsberger, B., and E. Reiner. *The Series HAR-ra: hubullu, Tablets XX–XXIV.* Rome, 1974.
RLA	*Reallexikon der Assyriologie.* Berlin, 1928–.
SAA	*State Archives of Assyria.*
SAA VII	Fales, F. M., and J. N. Postgate. *States Archives of Assyria: Imperial Administrative Records, Part I.* Helsinki, 1992.
SAA VIII	Hunger, H. *States Archives of Assyria: Astrological Reports to Assyrian Kings.* Helsinki, 1992.
TCL	*Textes cunéiformes du Louvre.*
YBC	*Yale Babylonian Collection.*
YOS	Yale Oriental Series.

COOKING AND THE
PLEASURES OF THE
TABLE IN ANCIENT
MESOPOTAMIA

There is nothing more commonplace than eating and drinking. And certainly nothing can acquaint us better with the representatives of a culture than joining them for a moment or two in these activities.

Since the dawn of time, every society has organized these universal, fundamental needs according to a certain number of givens, all unique to a given society:

——a deliberate, half-instinctive, half-weighed choice of foodstuffs taken from the immediate, or close, surroundings;
——a system of effective traditional techniques and procedures aimed at working with and altering foodstuffs, transforming them from their original state so as to make them edible and tasty;
——routines and rituals, perhaps even myths, to regulate the use of food, indeed, to confer a value upon food that goes beyond the mere consumption of it;
——and of course the amount and the quality of the food served, according to the status of those eating.

All of this, like other "invariables" of a civilization, is faithfully preserved and transmitted from generation to generation—sometimes altered, enriched, or improved, depending on unexpected changes or new preferences, but most often without any obvious substantive differences, as is true of those deep-rooted, unconscious rules that govern our lives.

Such prolonged continuity creates an uneventful historiographical relief, even in the view of those vigilant, but distant, spectators—historians.

For unlike other curious observers of a more or less distant past, historians are naturally more attentive and sensitive to high waves in the ocean of time than they are to a flat calm. So they seem little inclined to take seriously such a trivial, fastidious, and monotonous subject as routine eating and drinking. Their lack of interest has been attested by their eloquent silence.

Few students of history have been seriously concerned with the topic of cooking and eating in ancient Mesopotamia, or have been compelled to consider it a basic component of the civilization of that land, even though they have come across the pertinent documents and have studied or worked with them.

This neglect by historians is no doubt why, in the two centuries since the rediscovery of that venerable land, so radically and so long erased from our memory, not one of these Assyriologists, as they are called, at the cost of incredibly hard, admirable work through which they have become masters of the distant secrets of the almost indecipherable "cuneiform writing" of that archaic culture, and of the languages, dead or forgotten, that were spoken there—Sumerian and Akkadian—from documents that have been dug out of the abundant underground stores of the land and have brought to light its countless vestiges and eloquent testimony, has seemed sufficiently inspired by culinary subjects in the land they were exploring to have attempted even a cautious general presentation, as I hesitatingly did in 1982.[1]

I hope I will be forgiven, then, if I use a more immediately "anthropological" rather than historical approach here—in other words, one more attentive to the customary behavior and the deeper meanings of eating and drinking than to their vicissitudes within the passing of time. I have set my sights on that distant, multicolored, unexpected, and captivating tableau of the cuisine and the eating habits of those worthy Mesopotamians, who died so many centuries ago after obliterating, as if with a powerful beacon, the horizon, or future, of their eminent civilization: that Middle East of long ago, where some of our most ancient identifiable ancestors lived and breathed.[2]

There is good reason for the reservations of most scholars, just as there is for the indulgence I now request as I venture to break their silence. That reason is the almost complete absence until quite recently of any indigenous texts containing information about the most revealing and most fascinating subject in question here—the Mesopotamian art of cooking—that is, the customs and norms of the chemistry that was skillfully practiced within the confines of the main laboratory of eating—the kitchen.

The Mesopotamia we know is not one of those ancient civilizations that have so generously opened up their archives to us; it has not yet allowed us to enter that room, which we knew existed but was padlocked. The information those people left us touches clearly and often on the vast realm of simple foodstuffs; but apart from a few succinct, frequently hidden confidences, we have not yet derived anything from it that enables us to look over the shoulders of the chefs while they were busy in their discreet culinary workshops with their praiseworthy, but occult, metamorphoses of ingredients into haute cuisine.

For the secrets of eating and drinking can only be fully appreciated by looking at culinary practices, which cannot be discovered except through the detail explained in *recipes*.

The Oldest Known Recipes

The most ancient collection of recipes that we know of, the oldest cookbook, does not, however, go back farther than the end of the fifth century BCE. The first identified patriarch of cooking was a certain Mithekos, a Greek from Syracuse and a contemporary of Plato, who once cites his name. Being a "professional," he was known as "the Phidias of Cooking." He had published instructions to go with certain Mediterranean dishes, primarily fish, as Athenaeus recalls in "The Learned Banquet."[3]

Aside from a few fragments, however, Mithekos's book has been lost. So whoever truly wishes to consult the oldest well-preserved collection of culinary advice and recipes can only—in the West, at least—refer to the famous *On Culinary Art* by Apicius,[4] a well-known Roman gourmand, glutton, and gourmet who lived at the beginning of the common era but whose book, containing about a hundred and twenty recipes, and actually compiled three centuries later on the basis of notes left by that glorious explorer of sauces and stews. Antedating Apicius, we have not yet found any complete culinary text that might introduce us to the early art of preparing food, and to the preferences of ancient taste buds.

And this is true of the entire ancient world within our grasp: the Egyptians, the Hittites, the Hebrews with their Bible, the Phoenicians, and all the rest of them; we can easily find out *what* they ate, but not how they prepared or enjoyed it; their culinary secrets continue to elude us.[5]

For Mesopotamia, until recently, we only had one brief recipe, dating from around 400 BCE, for a sort of court-bouillon; and from more than a thousand years earlier a vague idea of the composition of some kind of "cake." How might we go back farther and get an idea of the particularities of the food, indeed of the haute cuisine, in that venerable land?

An unexpected discovery, as is still sometimes made in these archives, shook things up a few years ago, causing us, if we dare say so, to make a rather prodigious leap of two thousand years backwards: two thousand years *before* Apicius! Three cuneiform tablets, dating from around 1600 BCE and exhumed from the drawers of the rich *Babylonian Collection* at Yale University—whence the name Yale Babylonian Tablets (YBC) as they are sometimes called—have transported us to a time well before that of the venerable Mithekos. The complete texts and their translation are presented and discussed in my *Textes culinaires mésopotamiens*,[6] and they are cited or mentioned throughout the present work.

Originating in southern Mesopotamia, it appears, these documents, in some 350 lines, which unfortunately have not all escaped the normal ravages of time, contain about forty recipes, enough to gain some knowledge, at last, of the secrets of Mesopotamian cuisine and to provide a clear, honest account of the procedures and techniques—the "principles" we might say—that governed cuisine and taste at that time. These documents constitute an unhoped-for and exceptional contribution— the only one we have of such respectable antiquity—to the earliest history of eating, indeed of eating well, and it is a contribution well worth revealing and discussing here. It alone legitimizes the present book.

I saw this topic as a wonderful opportunity to delve into a subject that has been practically ignored and neglected by all, including professionals, but is fascinating for anyone who is at all interested in knowing humankind with its interminable and obscure past, its slow, mysterious progress. It allowed me to look into the most hidden corners of Mesopotamian life and thought, especially in a time that was at once so distant and yet so knowable, so obscure and so intangible until now, and about which we had as yet only formulated questions without answers, and formed only uneasy and shaky theories.

I took the opportunity to comb rather widely while focusing on this new information, to look beyond it and to present what we have come to know about the cuisine and eating habits among our most hoary ancestors, so that we may, thanks to the newly discovered documentary treasures, locate and identify another dimension of our oldest accessible past. This is especially important—as will become all too apparent— since everything in their daily lives, including their religious behavior, their concepts of life and death, were necessarily, and strongly, integrated into the cycle of eating and drinking. One can, therefore, through such a detour "of the mouth," obtain an original and solid introduction to the great paradigms of Mesopotamia's refined and intelligent civilization, which already shows signs of our own.

In this spirit, it seemed beneficial to me, when the subject allowed, to include the greatest number of details, citations, reminders, entire pieces issued from these early, little known, or quite unfamiliar ancestors that would enable us to discover some of their unexpected secrets concerning eating and drinking as they understood and practiced them, so that we might appreciate and taste things as they appreciated and tasted them.

To speak only of the Mesopotamians' thoughts and preferences would be a strange and annoying way of presenting cooking and eating, which were in no way abstractions but were concrete and very common practices, connected to just about everything around them. Nor must we ever forget that good historians do not seek the past with our own vision and experience, distorted by our own perspective, our "specific mentality," but as *those for whom it was the present* contemplated and dreamed it.

I have tried to extract any professional pedantry from this work, any scholarly and "intellectual" language, in order to render my presentation more intelligible—even if here and there parts might not always be completely clear: there are occasionally, after all, technical formulations that require a slight personal effort by anyone who is not a professional but is simply eager to understand.

I myself have *translated* all the original texts that I have liberally cited here; that is, I have *transposed* into our language a discourse foreign to it, inserting, when it was useful, unknown or additional specifications into the originals. Anything that in the present state of our knowledge is not even approximately translatable I have simply transcribed, or I have cautiously added a question mark.

I have enclosed in parentheses material that the text itself has lost through the ravages of time but is relatively easy or safe to reconstruct: this practice, though sometimes irritating, is honest and trustworthy. To give a rough idea of quantities, for which those folks had a system very different from our own, I have chosen to convert everything, even if approximately, into the metric system. I hope I won't be criticized for using kilos and meters!

THE FRAMEWORK,
THE REGION, AND
THE PEOPLE

First, who were these people? Where and how did they live, those ancient eaters and drinkers whom we wish to join in their kitchens and at their tables?

Mesopotamia ("Between Two Rivers," as this Greek name defines it), whose territory covered approximately that of present-day Iraq, has deserved such a designation for only seven or eight thousand years—a small amount of time in the scheme of our dizzying geologic eras.

While the successive quaternary glaciers weighed down on the northern hemisphere, the heavy humidity that infused the atmosphere at that time as far as the Middle East, and the massive thawing of immeasurable blocks of snow and ice on the mountains, had turned this long valley, caught between the massive spur of the Caucasus to the north, the Persian Gulf to the south, the soft undulations of the Syro-Persian desert to the west, and the piedmont of the Iranian plateau to the east, into a huge basin: the bed of a single enormous river.

It was only after the slow global drying that began at the end of the last glacial period some ten thousand years ago that this huge body of flowing water, no longer being fed, gradually receded, revealing a territory that became increasingly wider. The river ultimately shaped the terrain into what it has remained ever since: a large expanse of land framed by the same natural barriers and drained by two parallel flowing bodies of water that were fairly substantial but much smaller than their single ancient ancestor: the Tigris to the east, and the Euphrates to the west.

The soil of this new land consisted of a heavy layer of sediment deposited through the millennia onto a base of rough sedimentary rocks, of the same earlier origin, which would forever form the foundation of the silty and fertile land. This fertile and generous ground became the agricultural destiny of Mesopotamia in some sense, for Mesopotamian civilization was primarily devoted to agriculture in general—and, more to the south, to the cultivation of date palms—and with its grassy steppes, to the raising of both small and large livestock, primarily cattle.

While the sun was bathing the ever-widening expanse of the new land, immigrants from surrounding populations, who had already settled on the solid highlands to the northeast and the east, came to take advantage of the bounty and to occupy portions of the open land.

Thus Mesopotamia was initially formed and populated.

Covering a few millennia we have found only scattered archeological vestiges of the first occupants of the land, and we know nothing about the physical characteristics of those people—their likes, their lives, not to mention their speech, the cultural traits that they had imported, each group in its own way—or of their herds, their familiar plants, their more or less domestic animals, their still cautious talents and abilities. They lived in modest "village" settlements, independent and most likely isolated, and they survived above all by gathering, and perhaps by producing a bit of what they needed to live.

These conquerors of a still new land had not made a bad choice in casting their lot upon it. Almost entirely lacking in rock and associated mineral resources, with the exception of a little mediocre limestone and a few bits of asphalt, and lacking many plant species, especially trees, the land nevertheless enjoyed untold advantages due to the nature of its soil. It offered a wide, free expanse, welcoming and fertile, with two large rivers to feed it. But the climate was too hot and dry, especially in the southern region; and rain was too rare and too meager to sufficiently water the ground or even to contribute to the annual rise of the rivers, so as to extend and prolong their salutary effect. These were disadvantages that in the beginning did not seem likely to steer the land toward a future in agriculture.

All of that changed when the idea was born—at what date and under what circumstances we will never know—that irrigation could be developed and controlled better if flowing water were extended and mastered by digging canals joining the two rivers.

On an economic level the effect of this brilliant discovery was not just an extreme facilitation and enhancement of the work done for the production of foodstuffs: its impact extended even into the political structure.

To plan, dig, and maintain such artificial water courses demanded the mobilization of much energy, the gathering and the overseeing of many workers, and a closer, more directed, and thus more forced collaboration among them. The ancient settlements, insignificant and isolated, must have come together and established themselves into denser central groupings—the first "towns"—in order to manage their surrounding territory in a regime that was henceforth resolutely and durably monarchical.

In return for such labor, the earth was able to yield, and indeed did yield, as Herodotus (1.193) and Strabo (16.14) pointed out, "two-hundredfold . . . even three-hundredfold" in grain products, for which it seemed perfectly adapted; while the more generous presence of water favored both the fattening of livestock and the cultivation of date palms on the one hand, and domestic fruit trees and vegetables on the other. In such an environment, not only was there more than enough for subsistence, but there began to be a surplus, which in a manner of speaking happened spontaneously.

This surplus enabled the population not only to survive through the fruits of their labor and to want for nothing in their own territory but also to obtain, at the very least through barter, materials which, though denied them by the nature of their land, began to be indispensable with the progressive refinement of their customs, proportionate to their economic development: wood, for construction and woodworking; rough stone and gems; and minerals, primarily copper, tin, and silver. They had only to go gather them wherever they might be found in the surrounding areas: to the east, in the Zagros and on the Iranian plateau, indeed even beyond; to the northwest, in the forests and mountains of Syria and Asia Minor. Not only did the Mesopotamians have enough to trade and "pay" for goods, but, even though contacts with the representatives of other cultures were temporary, they encouraged mutual exchanges of concepts, experiences, discoveries, and technical know-how (one of our recipes, no. 16, was borrowed from Elam, a neighbor to the southeast), as well as images and ideas, proportionately enriching and refining the lives and cultures of both parties.

Things had probably reached this point toward the end of the fourth millennium BCE. It was then—as revealed by some several thousand small tablets made of clay (the most durable raw material in the land, and the one that could be used for everything) discovered in the ruins of the ancient southern city of Uruk, and on which rudimentary sketches of various everyday and often recognizable objects accompanied by simple signs of numeration had been drawn with a pointed tool—that for the first time in the world *writing was discovered*, that incomparable process for transposing, we might say, thoughts and feelings, for materializing them, fixing them outside of a person like so many independent and concrete objects, and thus communicating them to others, everywhere, in time and space.

Aside from a few small collections of signs or sketches that were apparently meant for the private use of professionals who were "learning their letters," rather like our primary grammars, these first *writings*, still in a rough state, appear from the start to have been accounting documents: their raison d'être was obviously to *recall* the content, the detail, and the numbers of transactions carried out or planned, concerning the provision or distribution of the fruits of men's labor. Such an accounting assumes a true economic abundance that had to be managed. And the appearance of writing thus demonstrates, in its way, that the Mesopotamia of that time, through the wealth of its exploited resources, had certainly become a land that was both organized and opulent—a true economic power, no doubt superior to the populations and cultures scattered around it, with whom it maintained material or cultural exchanges.

Regarding its southern region—roughly five hundred kilometers from the Persian Gulf—which was generally the most highly populated and the most creative area, certain data that were discovered only later but may be cautiously transposed to a period a few centuries earlier, enable us to view the population itself around the end of the fourth millennium BCE.

Whatever the situation of earlier occupants may have been, peoples of whom we have only archeological traces—in other words, who are essentially mute—and who we can only presume must also have left even a modest mark on the common development, two ethnic groups emerge out of the shadows: the *Sumerians* and the *Akkadians.*

The first group must have arrived from the East, from Iran, and settled not far from the sea, in the territory that was later called the Land of Sumer. They appear to have been completely isolated ethnically, culturally, and linguistically. Upon entering the region they seem to have cut off all earlier ties: to our knowledge, they never received any fresh blood and never even had contact with their own people, if they had left any behind. Their isolation would prove ethnically fatal to them. On the other hand, as a result of their earlier knowledge and progress, and above all by virtue of a surprising innate ingenuity, it seems that upon their arrival in Mesopotamia they were already quite advanced, or very quickly became so as suggested in the *Myth of the Seven Sages,*[7] and were in a position to educate their new neighbors, who were still in a primitive state.

In the latter group, we can reasonably identify the Akkadians, who had settled there first, it seems, in the Land of Akkad, above the Land of Sumer. We believe we know more about this group, insofar as they were Semites, members of a very ancient population whose distant descendants are certainly still living today, widely disseminated primarily in the Middle East. Their languages are still spoken there: among these are Hebrew, Aramaic, and Arabic. One of their first centers of settlement and dissemination, the most notable at the time, was in Syria along the northern border of the Great Syro-Arabian Desert, where they appear to have long been partially nomadic. From prehistoric times onwards, they must have been attracted, individually or in families or groups, by the extraordinary fertility and the relative ease of work and life in the Mesopotamian land, and we can understand their apparent plan to renounce an uncertain and mobile existence and to settle down to an easier life: with this goal in mind, they had only to follow the descending flow of the Euphrates, if only on foot, as good displaced nomads. Such a migration, which we believe began in the darkness of prehistory, subsequently continued uninterrupted for millennia. Not only did this enable the Akkadians to maintain culturally invigorating contacts and ties with their earliest kin, with their "roots," but they constantly received support from them—a considerable ethnic advantage, to which they owed their ultimate superiority over the Sumerians and their definitive predominance in the land.

When (probably beginning in the early fourth millennium, if not earlier), and under what circumstances the Sumerians and Akkadians encountered each other and then gradually joined forces are questions we will never be able to answer. But it is a fact that from their long and fertile symbiosis (the process, no doubt, was not always continuous and harmonious), there emerged something new, unexpected, and considerable—a new way of living and thinking, complex and magnificent, original and brilliant, which, given its later importance, we cannot simply call a highly advanced *culture* but must regard as a brilliant and luminous *civilization*, the first in the world, no doubt, to deserve such a prestigious title.

The Akkadians, at first "poor relations," certainly contributed their fair share, if at first a somewhat modest one. But their contribution was profoundly marked, forever, by the powerful cultural impact of the Sumerians—once the Sumerians, toward the end of the third millennium at the latest, had been forever absorbed by the Akkadian Semitic multitude, which had suddenly and once and for all become the sole masters of the land, and the brilliant way of life that the Sumerians and Akkadians had launched together, was preserved and developed in its own way.

It is not necessary to follow century by century the three-millennia-long adventure during which a simple "confederation" of small, culturally coherent but politically free states, each grouped around a "town," was first united (in the last third of the third millennium) by the famous Sargon the Great (2334–2279 BCE), king of the city of Akkad, into a powerful, but fragile and ephemeral empire. Or how, in the hands of the powerful Hammurabi (1792–1750 BCE), it was reduced to a smaller, less ambitious, but more consistent, and viable kingdom centered on Babylon. And how later, the kingdom was then separated into two, often rival, but from time to time allied states—one in the south, Babylonian, centered on Babylon, and one in the north, Assyrian, centered first on Aššur, then on Kalḫu, then on Nineveh, each with its specific customs and laws and even spirit, but with common roots, until the middle of the first millennium BCE.

It was at that time that Mesopotamia, conquered by Cyrus the Great (538–530 BCE), and incorporated into his huge Persian empire, began to lose its atavistic independence and its energy, which was shaken even more by Alexander the Great's conquest in 330 BCE. Next there was the seizure by his Seleucid followers and the Hellenism that then invaded, and Mesopotamia was ultimately finished off by the Parthians. Mesopotamia could do nothing other than die off and slowly fade from memory at the beginning of the new era.

This brief outline of the historical sequence is presented in more detail in the following chronology.

PREHISTORIC ERA

Sixth millennium	The region emerges little by little from north to south as a great lowland between the Tigris and the Euphrates. It is populated by unknown ethnic groups who have come from the piedmonts of the north and the east. Those groups certainly include Semites from the northern edges of the Syro-Arabian desert.
Fourth millennium (at the latest)	After the arrival of the Sumerians (most probably from the southeast), a process of interaction and exchange begins to form the first major civilization in the area. An urban society soon arises through the unification of more or less autonomous primitive villages.

HISTORICAL ERA (all dates are BCE)

Ca. 3200	Early Dynastic Period: invention of writing.
2900–2330	First Dynasty of Ur (Ur I), the dynasty of Lagaš: time of independent city-states.
2330–2100	Old Akkadian Period: the first Semitic empire founded by Sargon the

	Great (Akkadian dynasty); invasion of the Guti and the time of "Anarchy."
2100–2000	The kingdom of Ur (Third Dynasty of Ur, Ur III): first arrivals of new Semitic tribes, the Amorites.
2000–1750	Rival kingdoms: the dynasties of Isin, Larsa, Ešnun, Mari, etc. Old Assyrian Period: first rulers of Assyria. Old Babylonian Period (begins in 1894): First Dynasty of Babylon (Babylon I).
1750–1600	Hegemony of Babylon. Hammurabi (1792–1750) reunites the country in a kingdom centered on Babylon, which his five successors maintain.
1600–1100	Middle Babylonian Period: invasion and control by the Kassites, who draw the country into a political torpor, which favors a vigorous cultural development. Middle Assyrian Period: ca. 1300, Assyria (capitals: first Aššur, later Kalḫu, and then Nineveh) gains its independence.
1100–1000	First infiltrations of new Semitic tribes: the Arameans. Second Dynasty of Isin: ca. 1100, Babylonian revival. Battle for hegemony between Assyria and Babylonia. Even when the latter is politically dominated, it maintains its cultural supremacy.
1000–609	Neo-Assyrian Period: Assyrian dominance, time of the Sargonids (Esarhaddon, Aššurbanipal).
609–539	Neo-Babylonian Period and Chaldean dynasty: Babylon takes control of Assyria in 609; Aramaization continues.
539–330	Persian Period: in 539 Babylon falls to the Achaemenid Cyrus, and Mesopotamia is incorporated into the Persian Empire; Aramaization intensifies.
330–130	Seleucid Period: in 330 Alexander conquers, takes over from the Persians, and brings the entire Near East into the Hellenistic cultural orbit; his successors, the Seleucid rulers, maintained their hold over Mesopotamia.
130–	Arsacid Period: in 127 Mesopotamia passes into the hands of the Parthians, under the Arsacid dynasty. The land loses not only all autonomy but all contemporary political and cultural significance. Another era begins.

Even though drawn in broad strokes, we are not concerned here with a segmented, carefully labeled itinerary. What we will undertake in the present work does not deal with the realm of events; nor must the subject be chronologically measured for us to master it; perhaps only a sense of the great eras—if that—is needed. For it is not our goal to recreate, step by step, the *history of eating and drinking* in that ancient land, an undertaking that would be both chimerical and, as such, pedantic and useless for our purpose. In this work we will rediscover, viewed from above with a wide lens, *how the ancient Mesopotamians ate and drank:* their tastes, the application they put into eating and drinking in that noble and lofty civilization; the spirit in which they undertook and performed those activities; their preferences, discoveries, and routines in that domain; as well as the way they saw and understood those things—facts that, especially given the state of our documentation, cannot be examined within the scrupulous sequence of days, years, or even centuries.

SOURCES

In order to cast our gaze from such a distance upon the vast tableau that interests us here, that of eating and drinking, cooking and dining, in such a venerable land that survived for so long and died so long ago, where can we find the remembrances and the vestiges of that endless past, perished in oblivion? What are our *documentary sources?*

Out of their long hibernation in the ground of ancient Mesopotamia, one hundred and fifty years of excavations—leaving aside, for the moment, the huge amount of archeological discoveries—have uncovered something like a half million cuneiform tablets, inscribed in Sumerian or in Akkadian, which originated from just about every corner and every time in that ancient history and, when duly deciphered, can provide an account of it. The information these documents contain might concern news items about people's lives, private or public; their customs; facts and events in social, economic, administrative, political, juridical, and military history; but also about their multiple creations in literature and the arts, their knowledge of technical matters and technology, as well as their folklore, morality, mythology, and religion. And, of primary importance here, these documents can provide information about eating and drinking.

A triple misfortune contributed to the compilation of such a file: everything that happened just about everywhere in that land, throughout so many centuries, was not recorded, memorialized by its inhabitants, and put down in writing. Out of a selection of "testimony," not everything was conserved. And out of what was preserved, all—necessarily!—has not (yet?) been discovered. The result, which must always be kept in mind, is that for some periods there is an unusual plethora of documentation, and for others—more commonly—there are enormous unfortunate gaps. Our "history" will therefore never be complete; at best, it will always contain unfillable gaps.

Regardless of the period, the place, or the domain, the picture we can restore thanks to our documents will thus be a crumbling mosaic in which only pathetically small fragments of cubed briquettes will remain in place, everything else having scattered and been lost—documents relating to eating and drinking having fared no better than those pertaining to other areas of culture and history.

So we must resign ourselves to not knowing everything, let alone knowing it well, and must get used to this cloudy and too often veiled method of observation.

This reservation having been made, those who are interested in studying cooking and eating in ancient Mesopotamia find themselves first of all, as regards nutritional matters, in the presence of an often dizzying quantity of documents, from which they must choose the most relevant, the most significant, the richest. The majority of these documents appear at least to be composed of objectively food-related facts, dealing primarily with the subject of grain—which fortunately coincides with what we know about the nature of the land and what was grown on it there. If we look closely, however, the items are noted not always for their immediately *edible* value but sometimes for their value as *commodities:* the Mesopotamians, following the distant and long-lasting practice of bartering, maintained the custom of using grain as "money."

Here, for example, are the first words of a large accounting tablet, with text over four columns and 238 lines in all, created around 1775 BCE in Mari (it is not dated), and which records, in the hundreds, the disbursement of barley to certain individuals.[8]

1   **90 liters of barley to Sîn-aḫam-iddinam**
     90 liters to Ili-tukulti
     90 liters to Šamaš-taiiâr . . .

and so on, line after line. It is specified that all the people thus supplied were "agricultural workers" (*ālik eqlim*), almost all of them receiving the same amount of grain, although some received a bit less—60, or even 40 liters. Now this was not a matter of *provisions* but of *wages,* and the barley thus distributed represented only something of value, money of account paid as a salary to compensate services, and usable as needed by the beneficiaries, not necessarily to feed themselves, but to enable them to acquire other provisions or other goods as required.

Certainly, the importance that is implicitly placed on grain here, especially on barley, the most important grain product in the land, highlights the exceptional place that grain held in everyone's life and consequently in the everyday consumption of food, but we will never be able to deduce anything concerning how the grain was actually eaten.

Thus, in spite of their detail, countless pieces can be excluded from our file concerning eating and drinking.

Regarding these activities, however, descriptive accounts are not lacking. There are two clear-cut categories of texts. The most numerous, but the least significant, tell us *what* was eaten and drunk: we consider these to be *indirect sources*. The smaller number, but of much greater value, in our opinion, tell us *how* food was prepared and consumed, *how* people viewed food in terms of something to value and enjoy. These are our *direct sources*, upon which we will focus the greatest attention.

Indirect Sources

By far the greatest in number, and found in the most varied of contexts, indirect sources above all enrich our knowledge of "menus."

One of the largest collection of documents, rather exceptional in number and coherence, is provided by the palace archives in the kingdom of Mari, from the first third of the second millennium BCE. Those responsible for the daily meals of the ruler had recorded with minute detail the quantities of the foodstuffs, both solid and liquid, plant or animal, when used in the preparation of the "meals" (*naptanu*) of the king, either alone or with his "people," whom he had invited. Sometimes these involve unusual equipment; sometimes provisions that the person in charge brought out of reserves to prepare and serve. The daily accounts were then recopied onto larger monthly tablets to ensure verification of the balance and control over "funds."

Thus, in *ARM XXI*, no. 90:

(Receipt) 180 (?) small *kamaru* fish
For the meal of the king and his people.
Under the control of Šarrum-Kima-Ili,
The 30th of the month of Kiskissu.

And again (ibid., no. 80 undated):

80 pieces of meat (mutton)
And two "joints" of beef:
(Everything) received by the cooks,
For the king's meals.

Other lists are more substantial and detailed, in which various foods are listed, taken from the same palace stores. Here is an example, also undated, which will be better explained as we go along. A note: following the custom of the land, "bread" is measured in "liters," by the flour needed to prepare it:[9]

1   180 liters of (flour for) unleavened bread (?);
      30 liters for leavened bread (?).

This bread-making foodstuff, at the top of the list and much more copious than the rest, obviously represented the principal element of the meal, which was in complete accordance with the local grain "specialization."

Then drinks are listed, not in very great amounts if we consider the volume. Water, of course, was used, though not accounted for. A specific type and quantity of "beer" is listed, known particularly in Mari at that time:

10 liters of *alappânu*-beer

The four (little known) varieties of flour or semolinas next listed, made either from grain or from legumes, were each automatically intended for a specific culinary preparation and presentation (sorts of "porridges"), as is suggested a bit farther on (line 14):

5   2 liters of coarse flour (?: *isququ*);
      2 liters of fine flour (?: *sasqu*);
      2 liters of semolina (?: *pappassu*);
      2 liters of groats (?: *arsânu*).

At the end of the list, what one might consider to be "accompaniments" or "seasonings" are listed and grouped together.

      12 liters of oil,
10   3 liters of "honey,"
      and 2 liters of sesame seeds.

After which, following the accounting practices of that time, the author of the receipt adds everything up, category by category. And first of all—to give honor where honor is due!—the bread-making foodstuff:

In total 280 liters of bread (flour);

then the beer:

10 liters of *alappânu*-beer;

and finally the four types of flour in lines 5–8, assembled here under the culinary heading of *šipku* "porridges" in the preparation of which they must have been used.

15   (Everything) for the meal of the king and his people.

Analogous documents from other locations and other times have been discovered elsewhere, but unfortunately not in great numbers. For example, from the Neo-Assyrian Period (between 700 and 650 BCE and from Assyria in the north), we possess this fragmented excerpt from a large, very damaged tablet that recorded both the "menu" and the guests at official banquets. Thus *SAA* VII, pp. 154ff, obverse, column II:

3   . . . kidneys [   ]
    [   ] quarters of fattened beef shoulders;
5   10 large quarters of mutton;
    10 [fish] baked in the oven.
    In all, 6 heads of cattle for the meat (of the meal)
    6 quarters of [   ] meat, salted . . .

And a bit farther, in column III of the same side of the tablet:

1   Livers and hearts [   ];
    10 geese [   ];
    10 *item,* served warm;
    10 ducks *item;*
7   10 wild pigeons; [. . .];
    100 turtledoves, served warm . . .

A large number of documents, each with its own context, style, even its own literary genre, can thus serve as "indirect sources." To provide at least an idea of them, here are some excerpts from one or two "business" letters: we have piles of such documents from all periods (especially beginning in the last centuries of the third millennium), in which the correspondents, among other subjects of interest, could indeed touch here and there on eating and drinking.

Here is what was written, around 1700 (the document is not dated), by someone who does not give his name, to one of his "brothers," who was equally unknown, a fairly regular occurrence:[10]

3   [. . .] Good health, my brother! You know that for some time,
5   you haven't been sending me garlic, onions, or *sirbittu* fish [?, unknown]. . .
11   I am sending you Muballit-Marduk [also unknown, no doubt a friend or a servant].

14   Get for me, wrap it up, and have it sent (by him) for 8 grams of money,
garlic and as many onions, as well as *sirbittu*-fish (?). . .

It is possible that these members of the onion family often served as accompaniment to the fish, at least for the type noted here.

Around the same time (the letter is also undated), a lady Ḫuzalatum requested of her sister, by the name of Bêltâni:[11]

30   In the last caravan I was brought (from you?)
100 liters of barley semolina (*tappinu*), 50 liters of dates, and $1\frac{1}{2}$ liters of
oil; and they've just delivered 10 liters of sesame seeds, and 10 liters of
dates.

35   In return, I'm sending you 20 liters of coarse flour (?; *isququ*), 35 liters of
bean flour (?), two combs (!), a liter of *šiqqu*-brine . . .

40   There isn't any *ziqtu*-fish (?) here. Send some to me, so that I can make
you some of that brine and can have it brought to you . . .

Our indirect sources are not limited to such "business" literature. In strictly liturgical works, that is, texts regulating and codifying the cult of the gods, we often encounter documents concerning food, which was of course understood as being for the gods in person but, as with all the visions of these lofty individuals, was a simple transposition of the image, the behavior, and the needs of humans. We will later see all that these liturgical documents as such might provide us as regards the "maintenance of the gods."

We must include here those "private rituals," those "manuals of devotional life," the "hemerologies"[12] in which the devout were instructed, day after day, about their duties, positive or negative, with regard to the divinities, including temporary bans on certain foods, the reasons for which are completely unknown to us:

In the first month of the year (Nisan), the 1st, it is forbidden to eat fish or
leeks [similarly, the second day of the month; third, etc.].

Certain literary genres, indeed, those specific to the ancient Mesopotamians, are more helpful than others in providing the relevant information we are seeking here.

First, there are the *divinitory treatises*. Those ingenious people, who like just about everyone were anxious to know their futures, had discovered and profoundly developed an original and famous method of doing so.[13] They believed that their gods, responsible for and authors of everything on earth, and consequently masters of the destiny of each person, graciously allowed us to see that destiny in events and realities in the present. Just as scribes (in this land where the first writing was invented, a discovery that always had a considerable impact and resonated in all directions), who, in *shaping* signs—primitively the images of things, tiny sketches—communicated messages, so the gods, by continuously *creating* and producing that which unfolded before our eyes, in the world and in our lives, practiced a sort of three-dimensional form of writing in relief, and similarly sketched messages concerning our future in particular. One needed only to know the "code" for this supernatural writing in order to decipher it, an ability that was the prerogative of "diviners," specialists called *bârû* ("scrutinizers" of the "writing of the gods in things").

Reflecting this conviction, there were endless compilations of lists of possible "forecasts" based on continual research; these lists date mostly from the end of the third millennium. They include unusual phenomena, observable in the workings of the world or the life of every person, and were believed to be so many divine warnings concerning the future, bearers of "oracles." Since *everything* on earth was ultimately in the hands of the gods, was desired, decided, and "done" by them, and was thus able to convey their messages, *everything* that occurred on earth, in all orders of nature, could pass those messages on to us: the movements of the stars, the birth of creatures and their unique appearance, the internal anatomical appearance of sacrificed animals, and so forth. Some of these truly specialized divinatory treatises dealt more closely with people's everyday existence and thus provide us with very revealing, indeed unexpected details, even concerning food and drink.

Thus in *oniromancy* collections we find listed and classified all that dreamers might see themselves eating in their dreams, not only that which reflected the usual food eaten, but also unusual, strange, or disgusting things: plant or animal foodstuffs, meat or fish; vegetables and fruit; raw products or prepared dishes; cooked directly on the fire, or in water—and each thing accompanied by the part of the future that it unveiled, and of its divinatory significance.[14]

Here are a few enlightening examples:

5   If (the dreamer) eats the meat of some wild animal: . . . there will be cases of death in his family . . .
    If he eats the innards (of an animal): peace of mind . . .
3   If he eats the meat of a dog [a taboo, see below]: rebellion, not obtaining of (his) desire . . .
4   If he has eaten *arsânu*-soup [presentation of a grain]: [   ]
    If he has eaten pea soup (?): [   ]
    If he has eaten lentil soup (?): [   ][15]

and so forth.

We can easily see how well such lists can reveal, illuminate, and enrich our understanding of the daily routine of eating and drinking.

Another indirect source that instructs us perhaps even better in this
same realm, is found in a very rich, specific area of cuneiform texts,
which certain Assyriologists naively insist on calling "Literature" or, better yet, the "Science of Lists"!

Also indigenous and completely consistent with the genius of these
people and their vision of things, as if the juxtaposition and the ordering
(according to their logic, often far from our own) of vocabulary helped
them to understand better, more rigorously, the jumble of the entire contents of their material universe, those "treatises" appear as interminable
listings of ordered words. We find the names of things alone: nouns,
never verbs or adjectives. Sometimes they are arranged in a single column with the Sumerian terms alone; sometimes in two columns, with the
corresponding Akkadian words opposite, like bilingual dictionaries. Even
if the logic is far from our own, indeed, strange or hard for us to pene-
trate, it is clear that a certain logic presides over this classification. Let us
cite, at least as an example, the beginning of the most famous of these
works (it involves wood and trees), a true "encyclopedia" of the material
world, which must have taken shape in the first centuries of the second
millennium BCE: opposite each Sumerian term appears its Akkadian
equivalent in the right hand column (to which I have added its modern
equivalent, when known, in brackets):[16]

1	giš.túg	(:)	taškarinnu [boxtree]
	giš.kal	(:)	ušû [ebony?]
	giš.šir	(:)	samullum [?]
	giš.halub	(:)	huluppu [oak?]
5	giš.šà-kal-sig$_5$	(:)	taradû [?]
	giš.kín	(:)	kiškanû [?]
	giš.kín.babbar	(:)	kiškanû pişû [*white* kiškanû]
	giš.kín.mi	(:)	kiškanû şalmu [*black* kiškanû]
	giš.kín.su$_4$	(:)	kiškanû sâmu [*red* kiškanû],

and so on for more than 350 lines!

In this same "encyclopedia" alone, the last two tablets (the 23rd and
24th: *MSL* XI), containing some five or six hundred lines, have been reserved for the subject "Food:" food and drink are covered here in great
detail. This provides us with the relevant vocabulary—if not in its entirety, at least a great deal of it—even though we are not always sure of
the exact meanings, since in the absence of contexts we are unable to
guarantee the translation or exact equivalents of the words.

Thus we find around 200 varieties of "breads" listed, depending on the flours, the kneading, the additives, the flavors, and the cooking methods, as well as the presentations; some fifty dairy products and cheeses; more than eighty dishes cooked in water; and so forth.

Still other documents, sometimes more or less unexpected, which reflect other inspirations and motivations, also allow us to acquire a number of facts from just about everywhere in the realm of cuisine and dining, of eating and drinking, which might complete our picture. For example, we will read below the "menu," detailed in more than 70 sections, of a huge meal offered by the Assyrian king Aššurnasirpal II (883–859 BCE).

There are cases in which one hesitates to categorize certain documents as "indirect sources," since they touch upon the culinary domain quite specifically. To my knowledge such examples are not numerous, but we can at least mention what is called "infernal cuisine." This concerns a composition from the beginning of the first millennium BCE, still rather poorly studied and obscure in places, whose hero is a comic character, a sort of professional "clown" or "buffoon (*aluzinnu*) who, among other jokes, responds comically to the questions put to him.[17] When asked about the dishes he would prepare or would like to taste, depending on the season of the year, he declares, for the eleventh month (ibid VI: 10ff):

Mule dung with garlic,
And chopped straw, with sour milk!

And for the second to last month (ibid.: 16ff):

As a warm dish, donkey's bowels
Stuffed with dog excrement and fly specks.

For whoever can read it, that was a sort of "inverted cuisine," whose common and orthodox procedures (mixtures; the use of garlic; milk; stuffing to garnish the insides of the meat, and in particular a piece of the intestines: a distant premonition of our noble art of sausage making?) are stressed, and ridiculed at the same time, by bizarre, unexpected, absurd, or disgusting details. We are thus not far from our direct sources.

Direct Sources

These are the most relevant and important, the most essential, the most informative, since they are the only ones that explain the composition and the preparation of dishes—that communicate *recipes* to us. I have already pointed out how rare they are, but how pointless it would be, none-theless, to claim to have access to the secrets of cuisine in that land or anywhere else without such documents. It is helpful, therefore, to intro-duce them here, in their entirety and honestly translated for the reader's information, before explaining what they teach us, even if it will require a large part of this preliminary chapter to do so.

Before the Yale Culinary Tablets were discovered, we had only the two recipes (mentioned above) in our possession: one that had been re-stored indirectly, the other explicitly.

The first, which concerns a "cake" called *mersu* in Akkadian, is not actually developed as a recipe anywhere; but we can easily gather a few scattered, lexicographical or economic details of it which enable us more or less to reconstruct its formula.

The term *mersu* etymologically refers to a sort of "mixing" (*marâsu*) of a flour that has been soaked in a liquid; the end product is justifiably called "bread." According to the various, more explicit Sumerian equiva-lents, the liquid used in the mixture could be water (*a*); milk (*ga*); beer (*kaš* or oil (*i*), even "clarified butter" (*i-nun*).

Our "indirect sources" (primarily delivery notices, of the type illus-trated above), add a certain number of complementary elements to this basic operation. Thus, in Mari, notably:[18]

> (Received) 1 20 liters of dates
> And 10 liters of pistachios,
> for making *mersu*.
> Meal of the king,
> 5   The 14th of the month of Kiskissu,
> of the year that followed
> the seizing of Ašlakkâ by King Zimri-Lim.

The last three lines show how documents were dated then, as there was no universal era for chronological reference.

We learn through such partial notices that in Mari, at least, the task of preparing *mersu* was often conferred upon a specialist (*êpišat mersi:* "maker of *mersu*"), who no doubt possessed a secret technique for mak-ing it. We are also informed that large pots (*diqâru*) were used for mix-ing, and that to enhance the flavor and richness of the dish various complementary elements—dates, pistachios (see above), dried figs, raisins, apples (?), or condiments such as nigella (?), cumin (?); corian-der (?), and even something that to our palates seems somewhat un-likely, garlic—were incorporated into the duly blended flour mixture. Once the mixture was cooked—we know none of the specifics concerning the way or how long it was cooked—it could be presented as something like a cake.

The second recipe, published in 1933, among a whole collection of economic and administrative archives removed by clandestine excavators out of the subterranean chambers of the great temple at Uruk, and dating from around the fourth century BCE, is complete in ten lines, without any other information. Following a custom that was known at that time, this small tablet might represent a "rapid copy for immediate use,"[19] whose purpose was to make the recipe readily available to the cook, who must have been illiterate. He had most likely asked some competent scribe to transcribe the gist of it, having no doubt taken it from a collection similar to those that are revealed in our Yale Tablets.

The form of this recipe, which, in the interest of brevity I call "court bouillon," since it certainly describes something like that, is clearly in the same style as the recipes in the Yale tablets: an informed "master" calls upon a listener who is there to learn, and he speaks to him in the second person. The model, which is very ancient, is known to have existed since before the middle of the third millennium BCE, and was no doubt borrowed more or less from the style of the *Advice of a Father to His Son*, written in order to communicate a father's experience and teach his son to live wisely and be successful in life:

9   **My son, let me give you instructions, may you take my instructions!**
     . . . let me speak a word to you, may you pay attention to it!
     Do not neglect my instructions!
     Do not transgress the word I speak!
     The instructions of an old man are precious, may you submit to them!
     Do not buy an ass which bleats (too much),
     Behind you it will scream with an ear-splitting [voice (?)]
     Do not place a field on a road, it is disastrous (?).[20]

In the recipes the "instructor" has kept only what he wants to teach to the one who is listening, avoiding useless justifications. We will nonetheless see that at least more than one different pedagogical presentation was possible. Furthermore, and we will return to this, the instructor is content to impart only what is essential: the principal steps indispensable for the success of the procedure, without specifying the quantities, the cooking times, and other secondary information that is assumed to be known, as part of his job, by the "disciple," or that he would know how to improvise by himself.

Here is the text of the recipe:

1 The necessary amount of roasted ferul [?: *nuḫurtu*];
 The necessary amount of roasted watercress [?: *saḫlu*];
 The necessary amount of roasted dodder [?: *kasû*];
 The necessary amount of roasted cumin [?: *kamû*];
5 6 liters of water you boil for a long time with (raw) dodder
 You add a few (literally: "15") grams of cucumber [?].
 (Cook until) reduced to 1 liter,
 Strain.
 Then slaughter (the animal that will be added)
10 And toss it in (to cook).

It is indeed a sort of court bouillon prepared in advance, in which the meat would be cooked.

We should note that although we are only discussing *cooking recipes* here, there were other recipes known in that land involving other products: the fabrication of perfumes and unguents; dyes; colored glass to replace colored semiprecious stones; beer; the raising and training of horses. Infrequently and sometimes inadequately studied, these documents constitute a true "literary genre."

The Yale Recipes

Discovered, as we've already explained, in the cabinets of the Yale Babylonian Collection (YBC), the recipes appear on three cuneiform tablets.[21] Neither their format or clay, nor their writing style or "hand," connect them to each other in any way—they are related only by their content and the fact that they seem to have been discovered together. Together these tablets, which had been randomly scattered here and there some thirty-five centuries ago—judging by the paleography and the language—contain the records of some forty culinary recipes in all. The recipes are most often independent (they are usually separated by horizontal lines), and in general involve the same culinary domain; once or twice, indeed, we find the same passage repeated in different recipes. To make things easier for the reader I have translated their contents, adhering as closely as possible to the original Akkadian while employing the style that we generally use in cooking, including the use of a few terms specific to culinary vocabulary that are inevitable and familiar. I now present them all together. The great age of these documents, the fragility of their clay, and their long sleep underground have erased some words, which I've left blank or indicated with quotation marks when they could not be reconstructed. I have used parentheses around terms either guessed at or added for clarity. Brackets with space between them indicate an unguessable word or passage.

For convenient reference I have resorted to the following conventions: each tablet, for identification purposes, bears a capital letter: A for the first (YBC 4644 in the official Assyriological numbering), B for the second (YBC 8958), and C for the third (YBC 4648). The number in italics that follows these letters refers to the corresponding line: A *25* is the twenty-fifth line of tablet A, and so on. Since only B contains 4 columns of text, the number of a given column, in lower-case roman numerals, will be noted after the letter B, and before the line number: B ii:*5* thus refers to the fifth line of the second column of B. If I happen to refer not to the *lines* of a document, but to the recipe it contains, numbered as follows in bold numbers next to the recipes, the recipe will be numbered in bold face: A **4** designates the fourth recipe (i.e.: *9–10*) of tablet A.

Tablet A (*YOS II* 25) is of average size: 118 × 164 × 33 mm. It is rather well preserved, deteriorating here and there only on its obverse side; but it is often possible to reconstruct what had probably been written there. It contains, as is indicated by its summary (lines *74*ff):

> **Twenty-five recipes: 21 (kinds of) meat broth and 4 (kinds of) vegetable (broths).**

Each recipe covers only a few lines, between two and five. And each is preceded by a sort of heading, no doubt the technical name by which it was known and which served as a reference.

1   (*1*) **Meat broth.** Meat is used. Prepare water; add fat [   ], (*2*) mashed leek and garlic, and a corresponding amount of raw *šuḫutinnû*.

2   (*3*) **Assyrian style.** Meat is used. Prepare water; add fat [   ], garlic, (*4*) and *zurumu* with . . . blood (?), and (mashed) leek and garlic. It is ready to serve.

3   (*5*) **Red broth** (?). Fresh meat is not used. Prepare water; add fat [   ], (*6*) salt, [as desired, cake crumbs (?)], intestines or stomach; (*7*) onion, *samidu*; cumin; coriander; and mashed leek and garlic [   ]. (*8*) Soak the meat in the reserved blood, and assemble all the ingredients in a pot. [For the term "pot" see under "Hearths and Equipment," text at note 47.— Trans.]

4   (*9*) **Clear broth** (?). Meat is used. Prepare water; add fat [   ], milk (?); (*10*) cypress (?) as desired, and mashed leek and garlic. It is ready to serve.

5   (11) **Venison broth.** Other meat is not used. Prepare water; add fat (12) some crushed dodder, salt to taste; cake crumbs (?) [   ]; (13) onion, *samidu; cumin* (?); coriander (?); leek; garlic and *zurumu* [   ]. (14) Soak the meat in the reserved blood, assemble all the ingredients in a pot.

6   (15) **Gazelle broth.** Other meat is not used. Prepare water; add fat [   ]; (16) salt to taste; onion, *samidu*, leek and garlic [   ].

7   (17) **Kid broth.** Singe the head, legs, and tail. Other meat is used. (18) Prepare water; add fat; onion, *samidu;* leek and garlic, bound with (?) blood [   ], (19) mashed (?) *kisimmu.* Then, a corresponding amount of raw *šuḫutinnû.*

8   (20) **Bitter broth** (?). Meat is used. Prepare water; add fat [   ]; milk; cypress [   ]; (21) onion, *samidu;* leek, garlic, and *zurumu.* Bring to a boil, remove the cooked meat; (22) and stir leeks, garlic, *šuḫutinnû,* and mint into the broth in the pot; then add (?) *zurumu.*

9   **Broth with crumbs** (?). Meat is used [there is a probably an error by the copier here, who writes "meat is not used"]. Prepare water; add fat, *šuḫutinnû;* coriander; (24), salt to taste; leek and garlic. Crush and sift spiced grain cakes, (25) sprinkle into the pot before removing it from the fire.

10 (26) *Zamzaganu.* Scatter cut-up pieces of meat in a kettle and cook. Clean some *bâru* and add to the kettle. (27) Before removing the kettle from the fire, strain the cooking liquid and stir in mashed leek and garlic, and a corresponding amount of raw *šuḫutinnû.*

11 (28) **Dodder broth.** Not fresh meat but rather "salted" meat is used. Prepare water; add fat; (29) some crushed dodder; onion, *samidu;* coriander; cumin; leek and garlic. (30) With the pot resting on the heat, the broth is ready to serve.

12 (31) **Lamb broth.** Other meat is used. Prepare water; add fat; salt, to taste; (32) cake crumbs (?); onion, *samidu.* Also add some milk, and some mashed [   ].

13 (33) **Ram broth** (?). Other meat is not used. Prepare water; add fat; some [   ]; (34) dodder as desired; salt to taste; onion, *samidu* [   ]; (35) coriander; leek and garlic. Put the pot on the stove (36) and, after removing it, mash in *kisimmu.* It is ready to serve.

14 (37) *Bidšud* (?) **broth.** Other meat is not used. Prepare water; add fat. [   ]

(38) dill; crushed dodder; onion, *samidu*; cumin [ ]; leek and garlic, (39) bound with blood. It is ready to serve.

15   (40) **Spleen broth.** Other fresh meat is not used. Prepare water; add fat [ ] (41) Scatter pieces of "salted" stomach and spleen in the cooking vessel and add milk to it; (42) Some crushed dodder; cake crumbs, (?), salt to taste; onion, *samidu* [ ]; (43) bits of roasted *qaiiâtu*-dough *šuḫutinnû*; high-quality mint; mashed leek and onions, bound (?) with blood, (44) It is ready to serve.

16   (45) **Elamite broth.** Meat is used. Prepare water; add fat; dill; *šuḫutinnû*; (46) coriander; leek and garlic, bound (?) with blood; a corresponding amount of *kisimmu*; and more garlic. The (original) name of this dish is *zukanda*.

17   (47) ***Amursânu*-pigeon broth.** Split the pigeon in two; (other) meat is also used. Prepare water; add fat; (48), salt, to taste; bread crumbs, (?); onion, *samidu*; leek and garlic. (49) (Before using), soak these herbs in milk. It is ready to serve.

18   (50) **Leg of Mutton broth** (?). With fresh meat from the leg of mutton. Other meat is also used. Prepare water; add fat; (51) salt, to taste; onion, *samidu*; leek and garlic, mashed with *kisimmu*.

19   (52) *Ḫalazzu* **in broth.** Meat is used. Prepare water; add fat; salt, to taste; onion, *samidu*; (53) leek and garlic, mashed with *kisimmu*. Crush the corolla (?) of some of the cultivated plant called *ḫalazzu*, (54) Assemble all the ingredients in a pot.

20   (55) **Salted broth.** Leg of mutton (?), but no (other) meat is used. Prepare water; add fat; (56) dodder as desired; salt to taste; cypress; onion, *samidu*; cumin; coriander; (57) leek and garlic, mashed with *kisimmu*. It is ready to serve.

21   (58) **Francolin broth.** Fresh leg of mutton is also used (?). Prepare water; add fat. Trim the francolins, (59) add salt, to taste; cake crumbs (?); onion, *samidu*, leek and garlic mashed with milk (?). (60) Once the francolins have been cut up, put them into the broth in the pot, but they should first be cooked in a kettle [ ]. (61). Then return them to the pot. It is ready to serve.

22   (62) *Tuḫ'u* **beet broth.** Lamb meat is used (?). Prepare water; add fat. Peel the vegetables. Add salt; beer; onion; (63) arugula; coriander, *samidu*; cumin, and the beets. Assemble all the ingredients in the cooking vessel (64) and add mashed leeks and garlic. Sprinkle the cooked mixture with coriander, and *šuḫutinnû*.

23   (65) *Kanašû* broth. Leg of mutton (?) is used. Prepare water; add fat; [   ]; (66) *samidu;* coriander; cumin, and *kanašû.* Assemble all the ingredients in the cooking vessel, and sprinkle with crushed garlic. (67). Then blend into the pot *šuḫutinnû* and mint [   ].

24   Ḫiršu broth. Leg of mutton (?) and "salted" meat are used. Prepare water; add fat; [   ] (69) onion; arugula, the best chopped coriander, and *ḫiršu* [   ]. (70) Assemble all the ingredients in the pot, and sprinkle leeks and coriander on top. It is ready to serve.

25   (71) **Garden turnips broth.** Meat is not used. Prepare water; add fat [   ]; (72) onion; arugula; coriander and cake crumbs (?), bound with blood; (73) add mashed leeks and garlic [   ] (?).
(74) 21 meat broths
(75) 4 vegetable broths

Tablet B (no. 26 of *YOS 11*) is physically the largest: its text, spread over four columns, two on the obverse and two on the reverse, must have originally contained close to 240 lines. There remain somewhat fewer than 220, and a certain number of them are incomplete or damaged: some parts have completely disappeared, in particular at the beginning of column iii and at the end of columns ii and iv. The recipes—there are seven in all, numbered 1 to 7 —are much more detailed, filled with minutiae, and quite different from the rapid and brief style of A. They are separated from each other by two horizontal lines. In two passages we can note the curious alternation of speech style (i:53 – ii: 15 and iv:32 – end): most often, the one who is speaking uses a familiar form of address with the one who is listening, as is generally the case elsewhere, but then suddenly speaks in the first person, presenting himself thus more as a *model* than as an *instructor*. We will return to this peculiarity. At the bottom of the fourth column, over two lines, there is a sign on each line that appears to initiate some invocation of the copyist to two known divinities.

1   Bi: *1 – 49;* (1) To prepare a [   ] of [   ] or "small birds," (2) you remove the heads, necks and legs; (3) you open their bellies, and remove (4) gizzards and pluck. Then you split and peel the membrane from the gizzards. (5) You then wash the birds and chop the pluck. In a clean kettle (6), you place the birds, gizzards and entrails. After heating it, you remove the meat, (7), and wash the contents well in cold water [   ].
    In a clean pot, (8) you add water and milk, and put it on the stove. [N.B.: this last passage was smudged by the distracted copyist]
    (9) You wipe carefully the birds, gizzards, and entrails and sprinkle

(*10*) with salt, and put everything into the pot. You add a piece (*11*) of fat, from which the gristle has been removed. You also add (*12*) pieces of "(aromatic) wood," as desired, (*13*) and stripped rue leaves.

When it comes to a boil, you add (*14*) a little onion, *samidu*, leek and garlic, (*15*) mashed with onion. You also add (*16*) a small quantity of cold water. Meanwhile, you wash some *sasku*-flour; soak it in milk, and (*17*) once it is wet, knead it with *siqqu*-brine, and, being careful that it remains pliant, add *samidu*, leek, garlic, (*18*) milk, and pot juices. (*19*) While kneading it you must watch it carefully. You divide the dough into two equal parts. (*20*) You let one half rise and keep in a pot; (*21*) from the other half, bake shaped *sebetu*-rolls of 2? grams each in the oven, (*22*) and remove when done.

You knead more *sasku*-flour soaked and saturated with milk, (*23*) and add some oil (?), leek, garlic, and *samidu*. (*24*) Then, you take a platter that can hold the cooked birds, (*25*) and line it with the dough, allowing some (of it) to overlap (the rim) by a few centimeters [literally: four fingers].

(*26*) You then take the large container (in which half of the previous dough was reserved), (*27*) set that dough onto another platter and line it with the dough. You choose the platter (*28*) so that it covers the space taken up by the birds. (*29*) You sprinkle the dish with mint, then, (*30*) to make a "lid," (*31*) you cover it with the dough that you reserved in the large container. (*32*) You then remove the top cover from the stove, (*33*– *34*) and replace it by two (baking sheets?), on which you place the two dishes covered with their pastry dough. (*35*) When it has all been cooked, you remove (*36*) from the serving dish only the piece of pastry that will serve as a "cover," (*37*) and rub it with oil. While waiting for the meal, (*38*) you keep [a distraction by the copyist, who wrote: "you do not keep" . . .] this piece in its dish. (*39*) When the birds and the broth are cooked, (*40*–*41*) you chop and mash leek, garlic and *andaḫšu* together and add them to the mixture.

(*42*) Just before serving, you take the platter prepared with a lining of crust and (*43*) place the cooked birds on it carefully; (*44*), you scatter over it the pluck and (*45*) the cut-up gizzards that were being cooked in the pot, (*46*) as well as the (little) *sebetu* rolls that were baked in the oven.

(*47*) You set aside the fatty broth in which the meat was cooked in the pot. (*48*) You cover the serving dish with its (pastry) "lid" and (*49*) bring it to the table.

2   (i: *50*). To prepare *amursânu*-pigeon in broth, (*51*) after slaughtering the pigeon, you heat some water (*52*) and pluck the bird. Once plucked (*53*) [here the instructor begins to alternate between "I" and "you," some-

times teaching what he knows to the student, and sometimes presenting himself to him as a model to follow] (53), you wash it with cold water. (54) I skin its neck, and you cut out the ribs, (55) (56) I open its underbelly and remove the gizzards and pluck; (57) I wash the body and (58) you soak it in cold water. (59) Then I slit and peel the membrane from the gizzard; I slit and chop the intestines.

(60) When I am ready to prepare the broth, (61) you place the gizzard and pluck into a kettle, (62) with the [red] intestines, and the head, (63) as well as a piece of mutton, (and you place everything on the fire). (64) After removing meat from the fire, you wash it well in cold water, (65) and I wipe off the skin. (66) I sprinkle the meat with salt and I assemble all ingredients in the pot.

(67) I prepare water; I add a piece of fat, (ii: 1) after removing the gristle. I pour in vinegar to taste [   ]. (2) You mash together *samidu*, leek, and garlic (3) with onion; (4) you also add water, if necessary. (5) When these are cooked, mash together some leek, garlic, (6) *andaḫšu*, and *kisimmu*; (7) if there is no *kisimmu*, you mash (8) *bâru*, and add it.

(9) After removing the *amursânu*-pigeon from the pot, (10) you wipe it off. Then you [   ] the stove, (11) and stoke the fire [   ]. (12) I then roast the legs at high heat (?) (13); I wrap them in dough, (14) and I place the *amursânu*-pigeon filets on [the dish?]. (15) When it is all cooked, I remove the pot from the fire, (16) and before the broth cools, you rub the meat with garlic, add greens (17) and vinegar. (18–19) The broth may be eaten at a later time. (20) It is ready to serve.

3   (ii. 21). To prepare a bird slaughtered for a *timru* ceremony, (22) once it has been decapitated, you pluck the animal; (23) you wash it in cold water; you slit its throat (24) and take out its ribs. (25) Open its belly carefully, (26) and remove its gizzard and pluck, (27) wash them in cold water, (28) and soak the bird in cold water.

(29) I then split and peel the membrane from the gizzard; (30) I split and chop the pluck; (31) you disjoint legs and wings.

(32) The broth should be prepared the same way as that of the *amursânu*-pigeon. (33) Meanwhile, (34) you soak *sasku*-flour in milk, and knead with *siqqu*-brine, (35) with leek, garlic and cooking juices. (36) I then allow this mixture to rise. I place (what is needed) into a pot; (37) I also put in the gizzard, and the bird resting on its back.

(38) When the bird is cooked, you remove it from the fire.

(39) I then spread the dough kneaded with brine onto a platter (40) big enough to hold the bird, (41) and you place the platter covered with the dough in the oven.

(42) You remove the platter from the fire, and onto the platter you place (43) the cooked bird. You disjoint (44) the thighs [   ] (45) and [   ]; and, (46) using a string, (47) you truss the legs to the sides, (48) and tie the neck to the body, (48) so that [   ] doesn't [   ]; (49ff) [in a damaged passage there is mention of "roasted barley" qalîtu; then the word "pot" reappears. A dozen lines are lost, or unintelligible].

4   [From the end of column ii, through the beginning of iii, over some forty lines, nothing coherent or intelligible can be read. The discernable vocabulary is known: "pot;" "kettle;" various condiments; fat; gristle removed; one "stokes the fire" (13); "when it is cooked" (14); "filet" (?) (20). . . This concerns (21ff) the preparation of a bird called agarukku (211) to which the following recipe refers (30).]

5   (iii: 38). To prepare kippu birds in broth, (39) the same method is used as for agarukku-birds.
       (40) You open the birds (to empty them and carve them), and wash them in cold water; (41) then put them in a kettle. (41b) After removing from the fire, (42) you wash them well in cold water; (43) sprinkle with vinegar, (44) and rub all over with crushed mint and salt, (45) . . . (46) You clean a kettle, place water and mint in it (47) and (the bird itself).
       When you have removed everything from the fire, wash (the meat) well in cold water. (48) Then you place everything into a pot. It is ready to serve.

6   (iii: 49–end of column iii): [over only some fifteen lines, there remains only the initial recipe heading:] (49) To prepare kamkam-birds in broth, (50) the same method is used as for agarukku-birds. (51–57); [a few incoherent words].

7   (iv:1) To prepare a francolin for a . . . (2) You split the bird open, wash it well in cold water, (3) and place it in a kettle. (4) You remove it from the fire, and wash it again in cold water; (5) sprinkle with vinegar; combine mint and salt (6), and rub bird with mixture thoroughly.
       [Variant:] (Or) you scrub a kettle (7), place beer and fat in it; wash the bird well in cold water, and (8) combine all ingredients (needed) in the kettle. (9) When the kettle is hot, you remove from fire, sprinkle the contents with vinegar, and rub (10) with mint and salt. [Another variant:] (Or yet), you clean a kettle, (11) put clear water and the bird in it, and place on the fire. You remove from the fire, (12) clean the contents well in clear water, and, when dry, (13) rub well with garlic. (14) [Another variant, for the preparation of the broth] You prepare a kettle; singe the "white" meat of the francolin, clean it well with water, (15) and place it in the kettle. You

remove it from fire, wash it well with cold water, (16) and wipe off the "skin." [Another variant:] (Or) (17), wash a piece of beef or mutton. You remove it from fire, wash it well in water, (18) and wipe off the "skin."

(19) You place all ingredients in a pot, with water, (20) and add a piece of fat with the gristle removed. (21) You carefully measure some vinegar (which you sprinkle onto it), (22) and add, as desired, pieces of "(aromatic) wood," (23) and stripped rue leaves. When it comes to a boil, you add (24) *samidu*, leek, and garlic mashed with onion, (25) and put it in the pot. You then place the bird in the pot, and cook.

(26) When the francolin meat is cooked, (27) you crush together leek, garlic and [ ], and *kisimmu*, (28) and sprinkle mint onto the leg. (29) With these herbs [ ], (30) as the first time [ ] (31) with water [ ].

(32) [Another alternation of the "I" and the "you," from here to the end of the tablet] I then wash some *sasku*-flour, (33) and I soak it in cold water (34) and knead it with *siqqu*-brine. I mix [ ] in a mortar, (35) I sift it with a sieve, and I separate on the one hand (36) the larger particles; on the other, the smaller ones. (37) [Variant:] (Or) I combine in a mortar some [ ], with its *ridu* and its *egasilimmu* [ ] (38–39) like (?) to grind the roasted seeds; I sift them with a seive, (40) and I separate, on the one side, the larger particles, (41) on the other, the smaller ones. (42) [Another variant:] (Or) (I take) some coarsely-ground *sasku*-flour, with its *ridu* and its *egasilimmu*, (43) which I sift and put aside. (44) [Another variant:] (Or) some coarsely-ground white flour, with its *ridu* and its *egasilimmu*, (45) which I sift and set aside. (46) [Yet another variant:] (Or) I take, some light *butumtu*, or husked lentils, (47) which are milled for me: I sift everything with a sieve, (48) separating the larger and smaller particles.

(49) I cook these porridges slowly, each one (50) in an *assallu* platter, with beer in which "(aromatic) wood" has been soaked, in order later to add the porridge (to the meat on the dish). (51) [Variant?:] (Or [?] I knead coarsely ground *ziqqu*-flour with buttermilk. (52) I "butter" an *assallu* platter (53) and I cook the dough (thus layered) in it, spread very thin.

(54) When it is cooked, I rub it (with oil?) and set it aside. (55) Then I mix together *tiktu*-flour with beer in which pieces of "(aromatic) wood" have soaked, (56) and I pour everything into an *assallu* platter. I also add leek, garlic, (57) *samidu*, honey, clarified butter, and one of the above-mentioned porridges, and (58) I put the bird on the same *assallu*-platter. (59) Before removing from the fire [ ].

The following five lines are unintelligible and convey nothing to us; again they deal only with "porridge" (to accompany the main dish upon serving?).

At the foot of the column, one finds traces of the first words of (66) and (67), that is, two divine names:

(66) Nisaba [   ]
(67) Ḫaia [   ]

Tablet C (*YOS 11, no. 27*) is the smallest of the three (89 × 137 × 37 mm), the shortest, and the most damaged. It contains only three recipes 1–3, separated by two horizontal lines after the first, and a single line after the second. It is impossible to restore the complete text, but what is left of its contents connects it closely to the other two tablets, especially B.

1   (1) To prepare a *nin*-bird [   ], (2) you split open the bird, (3) detach its [   ] larynx, and (4) [   ], place it in a kettle.

   (5) After removing it from the fire, you wash it well in cold water. (6) You sprinkle with clean salt. Then you take a pot, (7) add water; (8) and add a piece of fat with its gristle removed. (9) You also add some vinegar, as required; some crushed "(aromatic) wood," (10) stripped rue leaves. (11) Then you mash together *samidu*, leek and garlic, with onion.

   (12) When it comes to a boil [   ] meat and beer (13) [   ] a lot [   ]. (14) You sprinkle (everything) with leek, garlic and *andaḫšu*. (15) Then you clean *sasku*-flour [   ] (16) and add to the meat that has been cut up and [   ] (17) pour it into the pot. It is ready to serve.

2   (18) To prepare (a porridge) of clear *buṭumtu* [an unidentified grain], (19) you take either a *sabiltu*-container or (20) a pot. In addition [   ], (21) you put [   ] (22) cold water in.

   (23–29) [are lost].

   (30) [   ] the pot [   ], (31) will be present [   ] (32) in the water and oil.

   (33) You put (into the pot?) water and oil, (34) and, when removed from the fire, (35–36) [   ], (37) [   ] some oil over the mixture.

   (38) As desired, you add (39) *tiktu*-flour, [   ] in the *tiktu*-flour of [   ]; (40) as desired, (41) immediately after pouring (the mixture) into the pot, (42) you pour it back into the kettle. And just before serving (43) you put it back in the pot.

3   (44) To prepare a [   ], for a *tamqîtu* sacrifice (45) after slaughtering it (the animal) and (46) removing the legs, wash it well in water (47) and assemble (all ingredients) in a pot.

   (48) As soon as you have put the cut-up meat into the water, (49) before the cooking juices have cooled ("rested"), you stir in *šuḫutinnû* and [   ].

   (50) When the cooking juices have clarified, with some *šuḫutinnû*,

(51) you (mix) blood and garlic, (53) which you scatter in the pot. Then you add some [   ] (53) into the pot.

These are the "recipes" we have recovered out of the long history of ancient Mesopotamia. They touch upon only a tiny number of categories of food: grain and flour products; an armful of vegetables, and quite a few meats—cattle, sheep, and fowl, both domestic and wild.

We possess no further documentation concerning the preparation and eating of any other foods, that is, just about anything in that land and its surrounding areas that could be eaten: fruits; fungi; eggs, even ostrich eggs; certain seasonal game and insects, such as grasshoppers; and, especially, the vast river and marine world of fish, shellfish, turtle, mollusks, cephalopods, to which it would seem—a curious but unprovable exception—the Mesopotamians were rather indifferent, at least at times, although we have evidence that they appreciated them and traded them in the thousands.

We don't really know, at least not explicitly, whether they had any true dietary taboos (perhaps only on certain dates); we do know, however, that there was never any question of eating horses or dogs, much less snakes! There is no known ban on pork: it was raised and eaten. But it was considered dirty, according to a Babylonian maxim:[22]

> The pig is not clean: it dirties everything behind it,
> It dirties the streets, it fouls houses.

Perhaps that is what discouraged those rather fastidious people, if not from eating pork, then at least from flaunting their consumption of it.

FOOD AND EATING

Let us now examine these sources to catch a glimpse not only of eating and drinking but also of the cuisine and dining in that ancient land.

Everyone *consumes* food: only a few people, who are more advanced or luckier, know how or are able to *eat well*. This axiom, familiar to gourmets, can be applied more generally in anthropological terms. For the distinction between what is edible and what one can ingest, appreciate, and savor is of primary importance.

The Epic of Gilgameš clearly points out the gap, of which those ancient people were well aware, between a "natural food," simple sustenance, available without any intervention by humans who merely gather it, and "artificial" food, which is planned out and prepared by people and is related to civilized and strictly human life, to *eating*.

When the harlot Shamhat, after seducing the "wild and primitive" Enkidu by introducing him to love[23]—not the "physiological," animal coupling with a female, but voluptuous lovemaking with a real woman, a woman "of the town," expert and lascivious, which thereby removes him from his initial way of life,—wants to complete the mission that had been assigned to her and bring her "civilized" phenomenon to Uruk, where Gilgameš is waiting for him in his high urban culture, she arranges for Enkidu to stop at the shepherds' dwelling on the way. Their way of life, though still "beyond the walls" and coarse, was essentially domesticated and truly "human" and could thus serve as a point of transition.

At the shepherds' home, Shamhat teaches Enkidu to *eat* and to *drink* like a human being, whereas *he was used to only sucking the milk from wild beasts;*[24] in other words, until then his food had been mere *sustenance*, natural and raw.

The shepherds then offer him their own *food:* their pittance, prepared by their own efforts and related on the one hand, to solids, *bread*, and on the other to liquids, *beer*. But Enkidu is unfamiliar with these products, for he has never encountered them on his steppes, in the course of his "animal" life. At first, therefore, he is perplexed and reticent:

> Enkidu did not eat or drink, but squinted and stared . . .
> Enkidu knew nothing about eating bread for food,
> and of drinking beer he had not been taught.[25]

That is why Shamhat, who has already tamed Enkidu somewhat, encourages him by placing into his hands the two products made from grain, universally eaten and drunk throughout the land, and equally necessary for sustenance:

> Eat the food, Enkidu, it is the way one lives.
> Drink the beer as is the custom of the land.[26]

So he obeys her, immediately realizing how good it is: that there is pleasure in eating and drinking such things, created in that way, and that they are tasty while also satisfying one's hunger and thirst. And he eats them with gusto:

> Enkidu ate the food until he was sated,
> he drank the beer—seven jugs!—and became expansive and sang
>   with joy!
> He was elated and his face glowed![27]

He was so content that while he was at it he easily took another step on the road from nature to culture, and set out to clean his body for the first time, taking a bath and using oils, before covering his nakedness with clothing, which was the final step that "turned [him] into a human" (awîlu),[28] in the elevated and complete sense of that word: a citizen, a cultivated man, an urban man.

This story makes it perfectly clear that, according to the customs of that land and by virtue of its lofty and civilized conception of existence, an urban existence, there was only one effective and appropriate way to sustain life where nutrition was concerned: eating bread and drinking beer, both activities being inseparable and balanced; both products also the issue of human intervention and efforts—indeed, in that land, of the primary and principal work of the human race, the cultivation of grain crops, so well suited to the nature of the soil.

The very terms "eating" and "drinking" both implied—although differently—the significant presence of a non-natural element, one that is "fabricated."

The verb to eat, at once the most essential, the most notable, of the two in both languages of ancient Mesopotamia, assumed the presence of bread. In Sumerian, it was pronounced *gu* (Assyriologists write gu₇); but its original sign, its ideographic transcription from the first days of writing, around 3000 BCE, was used, and would continue to be used until the demise of that form of writing around the beginning of the common era, as the sign for "mouth" ⟨𒅗⟩ with the sign for "bread" 𒉿 inserted into it; in "classic" cuneiform: 𒅥. In Akkadian, it was the association of the words themselves that revealed the strict relationship between things: *akâlu,* meant "to eat," and *akalu,* "bread," as if better to assert their essential connection.

For drink, things were a bit different. First, the true universal drink—water—was found in nature. And beer was, in fact, only a fabricated and refined substitute: it could not, therefore, by itself, be implicated in the act of "drinking." We have no archaic ideogram for drinking, but from the beginning of the third millennium BCE, following the model of "eating," the verb "to drink" was expressed by the sign for water within the sign for mouth 𒅤. In Sumerian, "to drink" was *nag,* which had nothing in common with the word for beer: *kaš.* In Akkadian, the distance between these words was greater still: *šatû* for "to drink," and *šikâru* for "beer," which opened onto an entirely different semantic area: "intoxicating drink." "Wine," as we shall see, came out of a later innovation and can therefore not be considered primitive in the land and in the vocabulary. The passage from *Gilgameš* cited above doesn't even mention wine.

At least in the more significant case of *eating,* in Mesopotamia the vocabulary itself implied an intervention by humans and their culture to make *edible* the *food* that by itself was not. As we shall see, this intervention, in Mesopotamia as elsewhere, involved subjecting food to fire—*cooking,* the primary and essential act in any cuisine.

FIRE

With respect to convenience or taste, a large percentage of foodstuffs that made up the diet of early humans was not immediately edible. As civilization advanced, there was a point at which it became practically impossible to eat a piece of meat, a fish, a handful of grain, or a beet, uncooked. Foodstuffs had first to be adapted to the psychological, masticatory, and digestive capabilities of the eaters, and in light of that goal a sufficient transformation had to be imposed on those foods. The most extreme and simultaneously most effective transformation always was, and still is, produced by cooking, by the intervention of *fire*.

With their first steps "beyond animality," humans were both marked and defined by their mastery of fire. The earliest occupants of the territory we are studying, having just barely emerged from the most ancient Mesopotamia, had already imported that treasure. And in that land, as everywhere else, primarily in the realm of eating but also in every other realm of life, culture, and industry, fire has always played a universal and irreplaceable role. This was true to such an extent that from at least the early third millennium BCE, fire was divinized in the land by the Sumerian name of *Gibil*, and in Akkadian as *Girra-Erra*. To designate fire by itself as a natural phenomenon, the Sumerians used *izi* (or *ne*—we do not know their semantic difference), and the Akkadians, *išâtu*.

Apart from "raw foods," mainly vegetables, and a few natural foods that were simply dried or otherwise prepared for consumption, all foodstuffs had to be cooked, subjected to the effects of *fire*, and it was primarily the cooking, that radical metamorphosis assured by the manipulations of food preparation, that transformed foodstuffs into edible *food*. Fire, in its various hearths, was at the very center of food preparation: not only in terms of its material installations or "kitchens," which could be large or small, public or private, but in terms of its general use in culinary techniques.

How was fire obtained? The process was obviously so common, known by everyone as an everyday experience, that to this day we have not found the slightest description of it, either direct or indirect, in that land where so much was written. Created by lightning or excessive heat in a land that was often torrid, but also by imprudent acts or excesses, fires, especially those that occurred in the huge cane or reed beds (the Sumerian name *Gibil* referred specifically to "reeds," *gi*, "in flames," *bil*), were frequent, sometimes catastrophic, and of course caused terrible private tragedies; but those infernos could scarcely serve as regular sources of domestic fire. We must therefore assume that if people did not extract fire from those destructive infernos, they must have been able to conserve it, gathering, with "a shovel" (*nêsepu*; Isaiah 6:6 speaks of "tongs"), the embers of an earlier fire, either accidental or intentional, sheltering them in some container or some ad hoc vessel out of which fire was extracted by the use of twigs or firebrands (*gizillu*, in Akkadian; taken from the Sumerian *gi-izi-lá*: "fire-carrying reed").

Of the two known procedures antedating the invention of matches to obtain fire at will—the rapid rubbing together of sticks or dry wood,[29] and the striking together of hard stones, flint in particular[30]—neither is easy to identify archaeologically, though the conditions for them existed in that region. They did have "flint," *surru*; and there was even a "fire stone," *aban-išâti* (not identified); but that word is deceptive: it was really only a "stone brilliant like a flame," but we have no details of its use, let alone its pyrogenic properties.

We may never know how the ancient Mesopotamians went about producing fire at will; but this gap in our knowledge is not very important since fire was present everywhere, even before history, playing a major role in the universal transformation of foodstuffs into something to eat.

What did they use to feed a fire (for cooking purposes, of course, leaving aside other uses of fire, in "industry," for example)?

We know that a liquid derivative of bitumen, kerosene or naphtha (*napṭu*)—or, as they said in Sumerian: "oil from the mountains," *ì.kur.ra*—had long been available in that area, and its flammable nature was well known. But people had never dreamed, to our knowledge, of "domesticating" it for heating or cooking purposes. In addition, "coal from the earth" was completely unknown, not even close to being geographically accessible for commercial use. There thus remained only one flammable resource, wood.

Although there were no true forests in Mesopotamia, there were still widespread copses of various sizes, and scrubland, but in much greater quantities than are found today, enough to provide plenty of kindling for

domestic use. There was also, of course, straw, hay, and other agricultural residue, and above all an enormous quantity of reeds, from the
canals and the reedbeds, mainly in the south—enough combustible materials to feed every conceivable fire, even an "industrial" one.

The ancient Mesopotamians had also learned (where? since when?)
to prepare that effective combustible material charcoal, called *pêmtu* in
Akkadian, which was used widely in cooking as well as in many other en-
deavors.

COOKING

Exposing foodstuffs to fire was not the only major process through which they were transformed. But it was the most common and the most widespread, as is easily seen by reading the recipes.

As in all fairly advanced "culinary cultures," several cooking procedures were used in Mesopotamia, depending on the nature of the ingredients being prepared, the anticipated degree and quality of their transformation, and the flavor to be given them. Each of these "methods" naturally developed into many different forms, perfected combinations and processes of varying ingenuity, which, to be carried out correctly, required equipment, especially "hearths" ("places of fire:" *ki.ne*, as they were called in Sumerian, from which Akkadian derived its general name for oven: *kinûnu*), appropriate procedures and routines—as is true of all professional techniques.

First, cooking was organized differently, depending on whether the food to be cooked was to be placed in direct contact with the flames or not: *direct cooking* or *indirect cooking*.

Direct Cooking

Direct cooking, either *roasting* or *grilling* or, with respect to grain, baking, was specifically called *qalû*. This was the easiest and most immediately practical method, the most spontaneous, though tricky because it required attentive supervision in order to prevent overcooking or burning.

The flesh of animals was perfectly suited to this method, much more so than were vegetables, for which I have no examples of a similar process. This "roasted meat" (in Akkadian: *šîr šuwê*, or *šuwû*) does, however, appear in our sources, much more frequently in liturgical than in "lay" contexts. For the latter, the great *Chicago Assyrian Dictionary* (CAD)[31] cites only one or two imprecise examples of "roast ox meat."

On the other hand, it is mentioned quite often in the rituals of the cult: in directions for the "meals of the gods."

We have learned that in Mesopotamia the religious cult was ultimately only the sublime transferral of court etiquette,[32] itself the generous amplification of the ordinary modus vivendi: the main form of worship was the service of maintenance of the gods, carried out by humans, whom the gods had invented and created precisely in order to procure for themselves, through human work, all the means for a glorious, worry-free life, beginning with eating and drinking. As we will soon see, in ancient Mesopotamia people were completely unaware of the typically biblical notion of holocaust,[33] burnt offerings, the "annihilating" cult that completely destroyed, through fire, what was pledged to the God of Israel, who, in his impassive transcendence, had no need or desire for anything. Mesopotamian religion was concerned only with presenting to its supernatural guests, who were decidedly anthropomorphic, true *meals* to be consumed fictitiously, prepared and served following the same rules, both culinary and ceremonial, that applied to the most highly placed of humans and, above all, to the king and his court.

While studying the rituals, we thus have the impression that "roasts," "roasted meats," were clearly preferred by the gods, whereas, given the rare official use of that method with regard to mortals, it scarcely seems to have tempted human diners. Not one of our recipes teaches such a preparation, whereas it returns frequently in the liturgy. In a ritual,[34]

> The cantor will then intone (the antiphon):
> "Let the gods eat roasted meat, roasted meat, roasted meat!"

Proof that this was not an empty exclamation, in the same ceremony the "*roasted meat*" often reappeared:[35]

> After preparing a serving platter made of gold, place on it (to offer to the gods) pieces of roasted meat.

Such a ritual predilection for grilled meats, compared to the almost total lack of interest in them with respect to food intended for humans, is intriguing. Without mentioning possible preferences (for we know nothing about them) in ordinary people's cooking, which may also have involved—indeed, probably often involved—roasted meat, less complicated to cook than dishes prepared in water, we must perhaps attribute its absence to the archaism of that method of cooking. It was, in fact, "primitive," rudimentary, if not "the first known" method in the darkness of prehistory,[36] before it fell more or less into disuse and in part was commonly replaced, if we are to believe our recipes, by other means of cook-

ing and presentation, whereas the conservatism of the liturgy had reserved it more often for the gods. Just because today, a little tired of the
more work-intensive habits of cooking with water, we have returned to it
with our barbecues and grilling, we must not deny the opposite movement among the ancient Mesopotamians. Here is how the officiant in a
ceremony accompanied by food offerings to the gods expresses himself.
Under the name, also obsolete, of Kilili, he addresses the great Ištar:[37]

> I have chosen you, and I offer you an irreproachable kid and worthy of
> your divinity: I have taken out its heart, which I've roasted for you, as
> was done in the past.

We should note, in the same text, another possible and parallel trait of
archaism: the use of internal organs, notably the heart and the kidneys.[38]

The more "modern" approach is perhaps why, among other possible
reasons, there is never any specific mention of grilling in our recipes,
most of which involve meat. In only two or three instances is a cut of
meat or at least a portion of it, placed in direct contact with the fire (obviously for the sake of flavor) before really being cooked in fatty water
(Biv: 14).

> You singe the "white" meat of the francolin [probably what we still call
> the "white" or the "filets" of poultry, removed from along the breast—
> the part reputed to be the most succulent] (on the flame [ḫamâṭu]); wash
> it well with water and place it in the kettle.

And again, for a "kid broth" (A: 17):

> Singe the head, legs and tail (on the flames [ḫamâṭu] before adding them
> to the broth)

A third example of this process appears in a deteriorating text, the reconstruction and meaning of which remain uncertain (B ii: 12):

> I roast [this time the verb is indeed qalû] the legs (of a pigeon) at high
> heat [fire? direct cooking!], (before adding them to the rest of the body of
> the cooked animal, to accompany it and serve it.)

These recipes do not really involve direct cooking, even in part, since the
main ingredient of the dish is cooked in fatty broth. They employ that operation—a culinary refinement unrelated to "flaming," but used today to
remove the feathers from the skin of a plucked bird—only to give the
meat that "burned" flavor they liked so much. A concern with flavor enhancement alone appears to have governed the choice of this operation.
In A: 31 ff, in which the animal being cooked is a lamb, not a kid, the recipe

is pretty much the same but does not use direct contact with fire. Kid meat, which has a stronger flavor, was thus considered tastier with a slight hint of "burning," given the preferences of the times, than was lamb meat, which was more delicate.

Although most vegetables, because of their texture, react badly to cooking through direct contact with fire — in our texts they are all boiled: A: 62–73; B iv: 49ff and C: 18ff — grain was often roasted or baked, either as seeds or as flour, and so were dried vegetables, which thereby acquired that roasted smoky taste so enjoyed at that time, as described in more than one document and by more than one word.

Incidentally, the average biblical character also ate qalî, groats that had been cooked over a fire, thereby acquiring a specific flavor (Ruth 2:14, etc.).[39] That term is found again among our recipes in the Akkadian feminine form of qâlîtu: "roasted seed,"[40] in the "porridge garnish" of a fowl dish (B ii: 49ff); but the text, in very poor condition, reveals little. Another presentation of roasted grain also appears twice in our recipes, in the known form qaiiâtu (B iv: 38), which refers to grain seeds that are roasted, then soaked and preserved in loaves of some kind; these "cakes" had to be crumbled (marâqu) in order to be added to the francolin broth in B iv: 38ff. Another time (A: 22ff), the same product, no doubt prepared the same way, was added to "spleen broth," in order to thicken it and to give it a burned flavor.

In order to ensure the appropriate amount of roasting or, indeed, burning, or until cooking was completed (there are, however, no examples of this in our recipes), cooks simply employed, as we still do today, an elementary, uncomplicated apparatus to expose foodstuffs to fire, or to embers, keeping it at a careful distance from the flame. They placed the meat on some sort of plate, rack, or screen made of metal or ceramic. Pieces of meat were skewered so that each piece could be easily manipulated and fully roasted on all sides through gradual exposure to the fire — an "archaic" form of preparation that still retains its effectiveness and ensures that the meat will retain its enjoyable flavor.

HEARTHS AND
EQUIPMENT

All methods of *direct cooking* could be carried out by means of a single, uniform type of rudimentary, outdoor "place for fire," containing both the flame and the embers. That was most likely the oldest culinary installation, the most ancient domesticated "place for fire," and there is every likelihood that it continued to be used: this type of hearth is ageless.

From sites in Mesopotamia, archaeologists have frequently uncovered rough models of such hearths, dating from every age, which their users had simply delimited by a border of soil, stones, or bricks in the shape of a rectangle or a circle, built up or hollowed in order to establish a firebed for repeated use.

Excavators, who often attribute a religious reason to everything they consider mysterious, first naively interpreted these hearths as places and materials of the cult, for "burnt offerings." An astute study by M.-Th. Barrelet debunked this theory:[41] they are, in fact, simplified culinary installations. Let us repeat: in Mesopotamia, people were unaware of the biblical notion of "sacrifice," and the practice of burnt offerings was unknown.

That was obviously the prototype of the universal hearth, archaic and ageless, the easiest to install as well as to use, for either the short or the long term, in both direct and indirect cooking. In Akkadian it was called *kinûnu*, and we have already seen why: the all-purpose hearth, which could be supplemented with devices or simple accessories, such as grills, skewers, or racks. The use of such a venerable multipurpose hearth has been preserved by nomads and campers up to the present day.

But, especially for large, permanent kitchens, such a hearth remained elementary and could not be used for everything. Perhaps (but we know nothing about this), it was what a very long time ago inspired cooks to perfect other models for "places of fire;" one, in particular, was used widely in cooking from a very early date. Our recipes, which don't say a word about the *kinûnu*, some dozen times explicitly emphasize another type of hearth, *which used indirect cooking*: the *tinûru*, so well adapted to multiple culinary uses that the "Great Encyclopedia," in the chapter on "containers" (Tablet X: 362), presents it, in Sumerian, as the "stove of cooks," *udun. muḥaldim*, the ultimate cooking stove. The word *tinûru*, probably already borrowed (the name along with the object!) by the Sumerians, though we don't know from which language or culture, in the archaic form of *turuna/dilina*, has a multimillennial history that we do know: it is found not only in Mesopotamia throughout its entire history but later in all parts of the Middle East and beyond; it is the Arab *tannûr*; the Iranian *tanura*, the Turkish *tanur*, and the Indian *tandur*.

Since it was built most often of clay, and hence was fragile, we have not yet been able to recover, even in fragments, any ancient example of it. But we do have at least two or three early images of this oven, which are barely needed, for it has remained to this day unchanged in its logical presentation and simplicity.

In its specific and invariable configuration it no doubt owed its existence—as appears quite obvious—to a precise need: the cooking required by one of the two great types of bread eaten in ancient Mesopotamia. This type of bread, whose antecedents escape us, coexisted with the "leavened bread" that we will look at below, the two comprising (we can perceive this already in the numbers proposed in the menus) what we can assume to have been the basic element of the local diet. It was served in thin loaves or thin, supple pancakes, made of flour that was simply moistened, kneaded, and spread out, without the addition of any fermenting agent that would make it "rise" or "swell."

It was thus prepared by flattening balls of dough separated from the kneaded mass, and applying them in flat loaves with a rapid movement onto the exterior surface of the *tinûru*, a smooth and very hot clay wall, on which they cooked rapidly from the heat of the wall. When cooked, they had only to be pulled off (*nasâḥu*) the wall and were ready to eat (see the recipe below).

It is possible, though we cannot be sure, that the very first attempts at baking this type of bread and at this method of cooking were made a very long time ago, either in still burning ashes, or on large flat planks that had first been heated by immediate contact with fire, techniques well known in prehistory;[42] nomads and soldiers in battle always used this method, and it bore the name of "flat loaf in ashes:" *kamân tumri*. In the *Epic of Erra* I:57, the soldiers, eager to go to war, proclaim that:

> The best city bread [which was prepared with care, leavened and raised]
> cannot compare with the pancake baked under ashes.[43]

Constructed "solidly" and attached to the ground, the *tinûru* itself was not transportable—unless it was destroyed! Thus it was used metaphorically to describe homebodies and stick-in-the-muds:

> Like an old *tinûru*, you cannot be moved![44]

It was built as a hollow cylinder a little more than a meter high and a little less than a meter in diameter, solidly anchored to the ground. The upper part was wide open, but normally covered with a removable lid. The lower part had an opening on the side at ground level to feed the hearth with fuel (which could also be done from above), and, most important, to assure a draught that would allow the flame and the heat to be regulated. It had multiple uses and functioned on several levels, as it were, depending on its desired use.

Sometimes, after lighting a very hot fire in the hearth, the cook would wait for the walls to be scorching hot and would then stick the flattened doughballs onto the walls to be baked, "detaching" them once they were ready. The "recipe"—or rather the procedure, for it is simple—is basically suggested in the first part of B (Bi: *19*ff). To accompany the "little birds," small rolls of "bread" called *sebetu* (a term unknown by itself, perhaps the "seventh" of a regular loaf of bread?) were scattered around the meat on its platter, which was thus decorated and garnished with the rolls, like those flaky pieces of baked dough that the French call *fleurons*, and the dish was then served to the guests. The composition and preparation of the rolls are explained earlier in the document (Bi: *16–19*). Once kneaded, half the dough was reserved to make a shell, which served as a container and serving plater for the cooked meat. With the other half (Bi: *21*ff)

> [you] bake shaped *sebetu*-rolls [which assumes that they were to be
> given a certain shape, but what shape?] of 2(?) grams each in the *tinûru*
> oven and remove (from the wall of the oven) when done.

The preparation of the reserved half, as well as a third piece of dough, which was kneaded somewhat differently (a culinary refinement), reveals another use of the *tinûru* and another way of cooking the unleavened bread in flat loaves (Bi: *22*ff):

> You knead more *šasku*-flour soaked and saturated with milk, and add
> some "oil" [fatty broth?], leek, garlic, and *samidu*. Then you take a plat-
> ter that can hold the cooked birds, and line it with the dough.

An operation that was to be repeated with the rest of the earlier-kneaded dough used in part for the *sebetu* to make a second sheet of bread, in the same shape but whose composition (yet another refinement) was not entirely the same: that dough would serve not to hold and serve the meat, but to cover it, making it into a "false pie," its shell and upper crust apparently not sealed together.

According to the rest of the recipe (**Bi**: 32ff), those two (ceramic) dishes, each covered with a layer of still uncooked dough, were cooked on the upper part of the *tinûru*, which was uncovered. Here, then, the dough was not applied freely to the burning-hot walls of the oven but was baked indirectly on the source of the heat by means of ceramic dishes. In that case the *tinûru* played the same role as that of our oven. As it baked, the unleavened bread assumed the shape of the dish placed on the heat, preserving its indispensable circular shape.

That new process of *indirect cooking without water* has fortunately left behind a few archaeological traces in the collection of some fifty ceramic cooking "molds" found at Mari,[45] most of them flat and circular, and all of them decorated in various ways with geometric motifs, human figures, or scenes; some were the height and shape of animals (crouching lion; fish), which gave an aesthetic touch to the cooked and unmolded food. Not one of them bears any trace of direct contact with fire.[46] This means that their contents, most likely some sort of dough, must have been cooked by placing the dish on a heated plank in the upper part of the *tinûru*, or on the bottom of a "domed oven:" there were vestiges of that type of oven in the region where the discoveries were made.

When molded dough platters of this kind were put into the *tinûru* along with pitchers filled with water, the *tinûru* assumed another function, allowing *indirect cooking with water*, or *steaming*, which we will discuss below.

Another type of bread, which required an entirely different environment for cooking, was "leavened bread." It was made with the same ingredients as the unleavened bread that was regularly stuck to the walls of the *tinûru*, but as the dough was being kneaded, a little beer or some leftover soured soup was added as a sort of yeast, which would make the dough "rise," fermenting and swelling to create a voluminous product filled with air bubbles that formed while the swollen dough was baking. By being cooked in this way, the bread became quite soft inside, but was surrounded by a crust of a different flavor.

This leavened bread could only be baked in conditions that were quite different from those used for baking unleavened bread on the *tinûru*. A different type of hearth was needed: an environment filled with hot air, so that there was empty space around the bread to be baked. This is what we call the "dome oven," in which, as is done in our own bakers' ovens," balls of dough were simply placed on the burning "base," which had been cleared of any traces of fuel.

More or less rudimentary hearths filled with hot air, *tinûru* and dome ovens made up the entire gamut of heat sources for the preparation of food. At times, several of them were used together, depending on their size and the size of the kitchens in which they were installed.

A full set of "kitchen equipment" was indispensable to make the ovens function properly and for them to be used to maximum advantage. Without burdening ourselves here with the multitude of utensils used daily to cut, slice, filter, sift, mash, peel, and crush, which the ingenuity of the users must have gradually dreamed up and created to facilitate their work and to improve their results, we shall concentrate on the most important among them. For the cuisine whose recipes we have found was largely based on *indirect cooking in a liquid*, involving two containers, which were exposed to the heat and would ensure the desired amount of cooking.

The first of the two, the *diqâru*, is mentioned most frequently in our recipes, and was well known elsewhere. Following the rules of cuneiform writing, it was sometimes written syllabically — *di-qá-ru, di-qá-ra*, and so on — and sometimes by its Sumerian equivalent, *utúl*. In the latter case it was normally preceded by the "classifier," also Sumerian, *dug* ("pot," "container"), which characterized it as being in the semantic category of "clay receptacles." Even though, depending on the times, the contexts, or the mood of the copyists, the term was sometimes used to describe metal containers, the *diqâru* was usually made of clay. It should be noted that the same sign, which was read as *útul* when speaking of the vessel, could be spelled *tu* (which Assyriologists then note as tu$_7$) when referring no longer to the vessel but to its usual content: the dish of a liquid base that we call "soup" and in Akkadian was called *ummaru*.

In other words, the *diqâru* ordinarily had to have been rather large and rounded, ideal for large quantities of liquid ingredients. The recipe for the "court bouillon" with its "six liters of water," was no doubt adapted for the *diqâru*, even though it is not mentioned explicitly. Unable to find a (rough) equivalent among the huge conglomeration of our own traditional kitchen equipment, and unable to identify any close relic of it from among the vast remains of shards excavated by archaeologists in Mesopotamia, I am using the term "pot" to render *diqâru*.

Its capacity, as well as its clay composition, no doubt, and its ubiquitous presence in the preparation of our recipes, must also have caused it to be used as an "all-purpose container." Here (Bi: 20), the cook uses it to "reserve" the dough he has just kneaded so that it can rise (as we still do), and later (ibid., 26), it is vaguely called a "large [container]." In Mari, in the first third of the second millennium BCE, it was in a "pot" that the "maker of *mersu*" prepared the dough. A pot was even used for mixing and, it seems, cooking oils and perfumes, some of which, when complete, bore the name of their "retort,"[48] thereby recalling their origin.

All our recipes using *indirect cooking with water* are prepared "in a pot." Although there was sometimes a choice of other receptacles used for similar purposes and no doubt of similar appearance, which are more or less unknown to us (in C: 19, a *sabiltu*; and in Biv: 50–58, an *asallu*), the *diqâru* was evidently the ideal container for the local cuisine.

We could not appreciate the subtleties of this cuisine, however, without taking into account the role of another cooking vessel, one that appears some dozen times in our three tablets: the *ruqqu*.

Also written syllabically (*ru-uq-qá*, etc.), it appears at least twice in its Sumerian equivalent, *šen*, which should as a rule be preceded by the "classifier" *urudu*, stressing the material of which it was made, but the classifier does not always appear, perhaps through the negligence of the scribe. Unlike the "pot," the *ruqqu* was made of metal, first copper and later bronze.

We have no data to assess its shape and dimensions, although we are inclined to assume it was smaller and less rounded than the *diqâru*. We refer to it as a *kettle*, which does not in itself necessarily imply a curved shape. It was, moreover, the material of which it was made that was important for culinary reasons: the transferral of heat through its metal walls was more immediate and better for shorter, more intense exposure to heat. We must remember this when questioning the alternating uses of the two receptacles recommended in our recipes.

INDIRECT COOKING
IN FATTY BROTH

In view of the culinary equipment that has been described—hearths and cooking vessels—it is clear that most of our recipes, those for meats, as well as those for vegetables and even "porridges" made of grain, would have been prepared in a heated and fatty liquid, hence in a pot. A: 28–30 can serve as a model:

> *Dodder broth.* Not fresh meat but rather "salted" meat is used. Prepare the water; add fat, some crushed dodder, onion, *samidu*, coriander, cumin, leek, and garlic. When the pot has been heated (for the necessary time), it is ready to serve!

Left to the professional discretion of the cook, the amount of time the dish was cooked is not indicated, and we cannot estimate it. But it is very clear that this was the typical method—repeated for the most part in almost all the other recipes—of *indirect cooking in a liquid: "fatty broth,"* done exclusively on the *tinûru* and in a pot.

Things are not always so simple, however, and in more than one recipe both the pot and the kettle are used to prepare a dish. For example (Bi: 5ff):

> (After peeling and washing the cut-up meat) you place the birds, gizzards, and entrails into a clean kettle. After heating it, remove the meat and wash the contents well in cold water. In a clean (pot) you add water and milk, and put it on the fire. You carefully wipe the birds, gizzards, and entrails and sprinkle them with salt; then put everything into the (pot). You add a piece of fat, from which the gristle has been removed. Also add pieces of "(aromatic) wood," as desired, and stripped rue leaves.

Since what follows begins with "At boiling . . . ," the cook would ordinar-

ily have placed the filled pot on the fire. He would then add a few ingredients to it (onion and *samidu;* leek and garlic) and let it cook gently for
the prescribed amount of time, which gave him a chance to prepare
the dough and the rolled-out pieces of unleavened bread, as described
above.

PRECOOKING

Cooking was most often done in a pot in fatty water. It is therefore clear that initial exposure to heat in a kettle did not constitute true cooking but only "precooking": the meat, placed on a surface of heated metal, was "browned," as we say—that is, briefly exposed to high heat to give it color, to firm it up, to extract its juices, and thereby to prepare it better for the final cooking in liquid—procedures that we still occasionally use today.

The old chefs of Babylon had perhaps discovered, in any case they freely exploited, this both subtle and knowledgeable method of precooking and browning meat preparatory to its final cooking.

It is certainly possible that in certain cases both precooking and the final cooking might have been done exclusively in a kettle. A recipe from A (26ff) might, at the very least, suggest this if we read it literally, and we have no reason to correct it as if the distracted copyist had written "kettle" while thinking of "pot." It no doubt involves a (small) animal, or a bird, whose name no longer means anything to us: *zamzaganu*.

> **You scatter cut-up pieces of meat in a kettle and cook.**

It is not specified that any liquid was to be added, but what follows suggests at least a small quantity indeed was, since some *bâru*, a grain product, was to be added, most likely in seed or powder form, and it could not have been cooked dry. The author continues:

> **Before removing the kettle from the fire [the kettle is therefore filled and must have been heated until its contents were completely cooked], strain the cooking liquid.**

It is also possible that when cooking was done in a kettle, the added liquid became much more reduced than when a huge pot was used. The insistence on "cleaning" and "scrubbing" the kettle after browning the meat in it suggests that a rather small quantity of water was used, since the meat would "stick" to the metal of the container, leaving residue there, which required that it be scrubbed carefully.

We are of course far from appreciating all the fine points of these various cooking processes, as the authors of the recipes always refrained from specifying the data that professional cooks were expected to know. And it is quite likely that simply mentioning the vessel to be used in cooking a dish tacitly evoked the methods and usages that were traditionally connected to those two vessels and their specific cooking capabilities, somewhat as a modern recipe might merely refer to a "casserole" or a "sauté pan," or a "frying pan," and without any further instructions we immediately employ the specific heating conditions that those containers require. We will return to this essential and complex subject.

FOOD PREPARATION
WITHOUT HEAT

Although cooking was at the very heart of this ancient cuisine, it did not constitute the cooks' entire repertoire. Seeking, as was their mission, to render raw foodstuffs edible, appetizing, and nourishing, they had more than one trick up their sleeves, and they could use methods that did not even require heat. However versatile those cooks may have been, given the extent and the variety of their work and their talents, some of the procedures and techniques that we will look at, though they may have been performed by the cooks themselves within the scope of their professional duties, could equally well have been handled by auxiliary culinary professionals.

In Mesopotamia, as almost everywhere else, *preserving* the food until it was served at the table was of primary importance. The often extremely hot weather, as well as the seasonal nature of many of the food products, reduced to a greater or lesser extent the period of ripeness and optimal freshness of foods, whether fruits, vegetables, or meats, too often rendering them not only unappetizing but repulsive. The flesh of animals and fish was even more fragile and liable to rot.

Granted, a large part of the vegetable kingdom needed no corrective treatment to remain as it was and immediately edible. Grain seeds that had been separated from the harvested stalks, vetch seeds removed from their shells, certain root vegetables such as turnips and beets, and almost all fruit with its rich sugar content, when duly processed and intelligently stored could remain in excellent condition for a long time without the risk of rotting. In the announcements regarding the "meals of the king" in Mari, "dried vegetables" were served year-round.

For everything else it had been necessary "since the beginning of time," in this land as elsewhere, to deal with the fragility of foodstuffs and to find a way to combat putrefaction, although how such methods were discovered and perfected is only too often unknown to us.

Preservation through Dehydration

A number of such defenses involved dehydration. Lowering the level of humidity in foodstuffs prevented them from rotting. Such a state could be obtained merely through exposure to air or to the sun. Around 1700 BCE,[49] a certain Gimil-Marduk, of whom we know nothing, wrote to his "superior," equally unknown:

> The garlic must be dried outside.
> Afterwards, you will send me a basket of it.

"Dryers" (*maštû* literally: "spreaders"), whose construction we are unfamiliar with, must have been used for spreading out fruit, dates, malted seeds, fish, or meat to dry. Through this process everything became "dry" (in Akkadian *ablu*, and in Sumerian *ud*), preservable, and edible.

In order to accelerate and consolidate the process, low heat was also used in certain hearths, and in particular in cooled "dome ovens." For example, this method was used to quickly dry herbs, used in seasoning as well as for medicinal purposes, which after drying were ground into a more manageable powder (*tabilu* and *šabulu*, which referred to the "drying," *abâlu*). Many "herbs" and condiments listed in our recipes must have gone through this process. The "dates from the oven" were prepared in this way, and they were considered quite good. It is possible that cooks may have hurried things along by cutting open, pitting, and halving ripe fruit such as apricots, those still famous *mishmish* of the Middle East.

This method was sometimes applied to fish, which in that climate could scarcely have been kept raw very long. The fish had to be gutted, the part most prone to rotting discarded, and the body split open, sliced, and exposed to the sun. The authors of the *Epic of Creation* evoke a rather banal image of this when—describing their great god Marduk, who after his victory over the fearsome First Mother, Tiamat, wanted to create the framework of the Universe from her remains (IV: 137)—they specify:

> He split her in two, like a fish to be dried.[50]

This method of exposing fish to the air or the sun, or even to a moderate oven, prevented it from rotting if the work was done well and in time. A divinatory treatise (*CT XLI:14* obverse: *10*), speaking of a fish prepared in this way, describes it as suddenly beginning to "move" and "lost its scales"—in other words, beginning to rot, in spite of the process that was supposed to preserve it.

It is possible, though to my knowledge we lack formal proof, that this dehydration process was used for meat, similarly prepared in thin slices and placed on a "dryer" outside or in the sun, like the *carne seca* of Brazil: *šīr mašṭê; šīru ablu*. I don't know anything more about it, or how it was used. Was it eaten as is, or cooked later?

Our sources don't mention this process at all. However, it does seem to have been used on a large scale to serve the entire community, reflecting in a sense what we would call "industrial" use. Toward the end of the third millennium BCE, a bureaucrat announced in a letter:

I am fattening the livestock to turn it into salted and dried meat.[51]

The foodstuffs thus dehydrated were then placed into "shaded" storerooms. In the "Great Encyclopaedia, we read of

the fish placed in the shade (*nûn ṣilli*),[52]

and even,

the meat from the sheep placed in the shade (*immeri ṣilli*).[53]

A document both informative and impressive is the tale by an excavator of his discovery in Telloh at the beginning of the twentieth century at the time excavations had begun again:[54]

The black earth . . . is marked horizontally here and there with large, yellowish, zebra-like stripes, four or five centimeters wide, which with amazement I recognized as fish (there were even some large ones, such as might have been, for example, tuna . . . , and cuttlefish bones were sometimes encountered), all pressed together, their skeletons, and even their skin and scales, still distinguishable almost everywhere. So these were not kitchen scraps. One would assume, rather, stores of salted or sun-cooked fish. . . . These fish, previously dried, must originally have been in contact with benches (on which they were placed and piled up for storage . . .) Their current disposition in horizontal layers, the very size of some of them, do not suggest that they might have been placed in vessels.

We possess no convincing documentation that describes the process of *smoking*—the preservation of foodstuffs by exposing them to the smoke of certain burning wood. A few passages here and there have been interpreted in this sense, as they center on the verb *erêru, urruru,* "to roast," which would convey such a process.[55] Still, it is more likely that the word designated a method of direct cooking, "roasting," but we have no further information.

Salt Curing

Another important, ancient, and universal method to ensure the preservation of foodstuffs, especially flesh, was the use of salt, a method as well known and as common as dehydration. Let us recall what a "meat packer" reported about his work:

> I am fattening the livestock to turn them into salted and dried meat.

And in a letter written somewhat later a woman named Amtiia gave the following order to her correspondent, a certain Nergal-etir, as unknown to us as Amtiia is:

> The meat you have available, cut it up and place it in salt.[56]

This was a natural and common practice. From the beginning of the first millennium BCE we have a short note in which the author, a literate man who was probably a "diviner" in the service of the king of Assyria and had signed some forty short reports sent to the king, explains to him that a certain Tamdanu, unknown to us, had come to him to announce that his sow had given birth to a piglet with eight legs and two tails, which, the author of the note specifies, citing a "divinatory treatise" that fell within his domain, foretold that "a king will seize the universal empire."[57] Since such a pronouncement, according to the custom, required an expert opinion, probably even a second opinion, the owner of the phenomenal animal, most likely advised to do so, declares:

> I put it in salt and preserved it at home!

The ability of salt to preserve food was no doubt known since prehistory, in ancient Mesopotamia as elsewhere. In a registration document from the end of the third millennium BCE, sent from the city of Puzriš-Dagan, the great center where a vast number of livestock to be used in the Ekur (the major temple of Enlil in Nippur) were brought and held, the sender points out that

> two antelope fawns, offered to the temple and intended (while waiting to be used) to be placed in closed storage, were salted; at the same time as sixteen antelopes, immediately sent to the temple kitchens.[58]

On the same topic, here is another edifying note, from around 1650:

20 liters of salt, to process the fish, arrived from [illegible], and they were indeed used (for salting). Done under the control of Warad-kinûni. [The date follows.][59]

Meat prepared and preserved in this way was called "salted" (*muddulu*, derived from *madâlu*, which means "to salt"), but it was also called *kirrêtu*, and *šîtu*. (There is a multitude of names that we know nothing about but probably referred to these methods or to how the meat was served.) Our recipes refer to this last word on four occasions: A:*5–6; 28; 40ff; 68:*

Not fresh but rather "salted" meat is used.

The cut of "salted meat" in fact takes the place of meat to be cooked in fatty broth. Once (A:68) it accompanied fresh "lamb?"; at other times, pieces of tripe—intestines and stomach (A:6), stomach and spleen (A:41), most likely, they, too, having been preserved in salt. It is worth noting that, at least twice (A:16; 42), recipes using "salt meat" prescribed the addition of salt to the broth: this meant—and it is not surprising—that before it was used the *šîtu* was "desalted."

We should mention that although the use of salt is not explicitly prescribed in more than half of our recipes, it is very likely that even without being specified, it must have been put into everything; we would need explicit testimony to recognize an even partially insipid diet in that land. Certain condiments, of course, might have been added as well.

We have no information concerning salting techniques. The terms employed evoke "sprinkling" (*šapâḫu*), light "rubbing," (*lapâtu*), or more vigorous rubbing (*pašâšu*, once or twice accompanied by an expression that reinforces the idea, and suggests a vigorous application). It is clear that in our recipes, at least, salt seems to have been provided in rather large blocks, which had to be broken up and reduced to grains. A commentary using *muddulu*, "salted meat," as a synonym for *šîru puttû* ("opened meat," in other words: "slit") suggests salting by slashes, inserting salt into each slash, a more extreme process than simple sprinkling or even rubbing the surface of the meat with salt.[60]

It is likely that other preservation techniques were used, employing mineral or vegetable products. For example, a lexicographical text points out a *marru* fish that is "bitter," "sour," or even "acrid," which might have been the result of a process intended to preserve its meat by using some drug, unknown to us and of a particular acidic flavor.[61] But we know nothing about this.

There has been some speculation about the use of pickling (*siqqu*) in the preservation of food, at least where fish is concerned. But there is nothing that describes such a process or, frankly speaking, even suggests it. On the contrary, *siqqu-* pickling was itself made out of fish, or shellfish, or even grasshoppers, which were abundantly salted and then left awhile to partially decompose. It was dropped into a stew, like the *garum* of the Romans[62] and the *pissalà* of Nice. But it was meant to be eaten and was not used for preservation; our recipes stress this clearly. The "*siqqu*-fish" (*nûn siqqî*), listed at the beginning of some recipes,[63] was not "pickled fish" but was "seasoned with pickling," which, moreover, did not preclude its nutritional possibilities.

Preservation Using Oil

It is possible that people had long been aware of the ability of fatty substances in a liquid state, primarily oil, to completely isolate the foodstuffs that are immersed in them and thereby to ensure their preservation. A very old economic document, from around 2400 BCE,[64] recorded some "hundred and fifty baskets of fish," that were going to be immersed and thus preserved in oil. Our documentation on this topic is rather sparse, however, which does not mean that the practice was unknown or even rare.

Preservation Using Cold and Ice

In such a warm region we should not consider refrigeration too seriously. All the same, we do know that small quantities of snow or ice were brought back during winter from the north and the east and were stored. We even know that people collected and piled up hailstones following a great hailstorm and stored them underground in straw, keeping them long enough to cool drinks, most likely for the sole use of the great of that world or the other. But these "iceboxes" (*bît surîpi,* "ice room") were never used to preserve anything else; they had a very specific and restricted use. Ancient Mesopotamia had no prototype of our refrigerators.

Preservation and Cuisine: Stored "Bread"

Most of these methods for preserving foodstuffs did not belong exclusively to the realm of culinary techniques, or exclusively to the work and professional responsibility of cooks, as suggested below. It was the job of auxiliary workers to produce, gather, and store the foodstuffs that would later be cooked and served; they were in charge of lactic preservation, which, if it failed to safeguard the milk, at least produced its derivatives—

cream, butter, and cheese—which were mainly the responsibility of those who raised livestock. But all these workers, who contributed to the preservation of foodstuffs to render them not only edible but appetizing, revolved fairly closely within the orbit of the cooks, so they deserve mention here.

A certain number of preservation techniques or tricks-of-the-trade relating specifically to bread and to its multiple preparations can, in fact, be called strictly culinary. We would describe them as the *paracuisine of bread-making*, without, however, bringing up all the practical problems raised by what truly was the basic food of that land.

What we call a "bakery" existed everywhere and even held a place of honor, but it never had the status of an institution, or even an existence outside the kitchen, as has already no doubt been surmised. Only the words that express the essence of each individual activity were distinct: *bašâlu*, used for the cooking of food, and *epû* for that of bread.

The processing of a certain number of grain derivatives so as to preserve them for either immediate consumption or later use can therefore legitimately be attributed, if not to the culinary realm itself, at least to the activity of the cooks. We refer to the preparation, noted throughout our texts, of what we might call the "reserve breads," which have already been (briefly) mentioned.

Moistened seeds that were sometimes exposed to low heat and left to sit in that way until malted, or removed beforehand, with or without the addition of flavor-enhancing elements, were molded (did the "brick mold," so widely used since the dawn of time, give ideas to breadmakers?) or shaped into chunks, patties, small loaves, or, if you will, in view of their size, large "cakes" made of seeds that had already been modified through soaking and had coagulated raw, either flavored or malted with a sweet taste. These "cakes" were prepared not only in the home but on an "industrial" level; a lengthy account from the middle of the second millennium BCE, at Nuzi (then the capital of a province in central Mesopotamia), records the single delivery of 5,600 of these products![65]

At least two categories of them are highlighted in our recipes, which is why they must be mentioned. One is widely known: it is called "beer bread" (*bappiru*, from the Sumerian *bappir*), thus wrongly reducing the scope of its use. It, too, was soaked for a time in water, either cold or lukewarm, plain or with "spices" added, was then heated in the oven up to the point of malting, and was then dried and shaped into small blocks that could either be kept as such to be used at a later time, notably for brewing beer, or stored to be consumed on the spot, or transported elsewhere, the way our "biscuits" were in the past.

In a recipe for meat broth (A:23–25), *bappiru* had to be "crumbled" (*ḫašâlu*), then "sifted" (*napû*), so that only the smallest (?) crumbs remained, which were then "sprinkled" into the broth. The name of the dish in question, *pašrûtu* (which evokes an idea of "resolving into its elements," or "crumbling"-*pašaru*), may have been derived from that process. The culinary role of *bappiru* used in this way, once its crumbs had melted in the heated liquid, was to incorporate its own nutritional value into the dish, to add its flavor to that of the meat and its garnish, and to thicken the broth through its property as "thickener," a use we still appreciate, especially in our veloutés and sauces.

Although it had a completely different name, one product in our recipes seems to have played a role similar to that of *bappiru* and is thus comparable to it. It is used in the plural, *risâtu*, the singular form being *risittu*. Both words, rather rare and little known, through their semantic structure evoke the idea of "wetting," or "soaking" (*rasânu*). The word could thus refer to a sort of "bread," similar to *bappiru*, although we cannot really see the difference between them. No doubt it would have produced a comparable effect in the broth into which it was added (A: 6; 12; 32; 42; 48; 59; 72), an effect we cannot describe precisely.

It is possible that *qaiiâtu* and *qalîtu*, which we have already seen in our discussion of roasted grain, were used more or less along the same lines as *bappiru* and *risnâtu*. They, too, were in the shape of "loaves" or large "cakes" made of variously processed and coagulated seeds (A:43; Biv:38 and 60, on the one hand; and i:49? and 50 on the other), since it is recommended that the cook "grind" or "crush" them (*marâqu*) before using them, and not throw them in a block into the broth, which would have altered the appearance of the broth. Thus ground, they were clearly used not only as a "thickener" and as flavoring but, in this instance, to add a desired "burned" flavor to the broth.

We know nothing, or almost nothing, about these products or similar ones, such as *bârû* (A:26; and Bii:8), a sort of grain or grain product (close to wheat, for which *bârû* was perhaps a name), which was also added to broth. According to Bii:8, it seems to have had a consistency, if not a taste, similar to that of *kisimmu*, a milk product. And no doubt there were others that our recipes do not mention or that are concealed under poorly written or unclear words. They all had their roles in what was eaten and drunk, as did condiments and spices, which we will look at below, and therefore all belonged to the realm of Mesopotamian cuisine.

COOKING WITH HEAT

Most food preparation concludes with cooking. In other words, to be rendered both edible and appetizing, most foodstuffs are ultimately subjected to heat. Here we have reached a decisive point.

Fortunately our purpose does not force us to adhere to the literal meanings of each of our recipes, as if to offer a sort of cookbook of Mesopotamian cuisine. Such a manual would be effete and fastidious, and, moreover almost unthinkable. Rather, through our "sources" we are only seeking an overview that highlights the originality of that cuisine—even though, necessarily, it shares characteristics with others.

Thus we are struck first by the fact that those early cooks, in the exercise of their profession, regularly proceeded as we do by way of three logical stages. First, they had to *prepare* the food to be cooked. Then, and this was the crucial moment, they *cooked it*. Finally, they sought to *serve* it to guests in the most nutritious and appetizing way possible.

Preparation

Neither the choice of the foods to be cooked, nor that of the type of meat and its cut, where a large animal such as a sheep (Bi:*23*) or a deer (A:*11*) was concerned, was apparently among the responsibilities of the cook; those choices were made by the organizer of the meal, the person who, absent from our recipes, always remains in the wings. But it was necessarily the cook who prepared the ingredients.

Tablet A, which immediately strikes the reader of its twenty-five recipes by its conciseness and the lack of interest it shows in whatever was not specifically culinary, essentially ignores preparatory details. With respect to vegetables, the most that is recommended is that they be "peeled" (*šamāṭu* A:*62*).

The recipe for the unknown *zamzaganu*, in A:*26*ff, directing the cook to scatter (*sarâqu*) the meat into the broth, thus implies that it should first be cut up into small pieces, which will cook more quickly and will be easier to chew; the same word and the same procedure is found regarding the "salted spleen" of A:41. In A:47 the pigeon must be "opened into two" (*parâsu*) before being cooked, not only, no doubt, to gut it, but to spread it out flat, which would make it to cook more rapidly and completely, a technique we still practice today. In A:58, which deals with rather small birds, similar to "francolins," the word *rakâsu* is emphasized. It primarily means "to tie together" (also in Bii:47) but also "to arrange things together, in a definite order," and, more simply and generally, depending on the context, "to ready" or, as we say in the vocabulary of cuisine, "to dress" or "to trim," which in this case needs no further specifications since it falls within the scope of the cook's technical know-how. We must therefore not interpret this word as meaning, as it does in Bii:47, that the cook was supposed to roll and tie up the francolins before they were cooked, as we do today with paupiettes of veal, for example.

No doubt the cooks included among these preparations the "passing onto the flame" of the inedible parts (head, tail, and legs) of the kid (A:17; comp again Biv:14), the end result of which we have described above.

One of the principal objectives of these preliminaries, no doubt, was to discard everything that was considered inedible, disagreeable, or without nutritive value, so that only the most substantial and appetizing food would be served.

In C:2ff, if the cook (opened?) the bird to be cooked, it was to remove its larynx, which was inedible. According to the other meat-based recipe on the same tablet (C:44ff), which no doubt involved a (small) animal, the cook must first "take off its fur," then remove its feet, always according to the great culinary law just recalled, that only the highest-quality food, that which is easiest to chew, should be served.

In contrast to A and C with their spare style, B dispenses a great deal of information and specifications concerning the culinary preparation of what was to be eaten. Unlike the lost beginnings of recipes 4 and 6, those of 1 (i:1ff), 2 (i:50ff) and 3 (ii:21ff) omit nothing regarding the required preparation of the birds to be cooked. Let us look at the most detailed passage (Bii:21ff):

> To prepare a bird slaughtered for a *timru* ceremony, once decapitated [to kill it? But the head, although it was cooked in the pot to contribute flavor, was not considered edible], you pluck the animal and wash it in cold water. You slit its throat and take out its ribs. [Again, the rule of serving only what is edible and tasty; so the rib cage would have been removed.] Open its belly carefully, remove the gizzard and the pluck, wash them in cold water, and soak the bird in cold water. I then split

[here "you" and "I" alternate] the gizzard, and peel it [the interior membrane, which is completely inedible, is removed]. I split and chop the
pluck [which will be cooked and eaten cut up]; and you disjoint [so as to
exclude them from the dish] the legs and wings.

This is how the animal was prepared to be cooked.

Without lingering in front of this carnage, it does raise at least one
question about something that seems a bit strange to us: What was the
purpose of those repeated soakings and washings of the meat before
cooking it? In the short passage just cited (A makes no mention of it, and
C touches on it very briefly on only two occasions: in 5 and 46), it is repeated three times. The cook often had to soak an ingredient in cold water, or even "wash" it, before cooking it. We are not used to these require-
ments, for which, however, there must have been good reasons.

First, Mesopotamian cooks were already aware of the use of warm
water for "plucking" (kapâru) the bird: this is what the cook is invited to
do in Bi:51 ff.

Also, we still follow the custom of letting a piece of raw meat soak for
a moment in cold water to firm it up and thus enhance its texture in cooking (Bi:57ff; ii:28).

Then, in the presence of the bird to be cooked, duly dressed at the
cost of somewhat bloody operations, we can understand that there might
have been a concern, not with "hygiene" per se, but at the very least with
cleanliness. The Mesopotamians must have washed their hands before
sitting down at the table (Dialogue of Pessimism, 10 and 54, in J. Bottéro,
Mesopotamia, pp. 253, 255; see also last paragraph of "Sources," above).
There is no reason to seek any other explanation, least of all one that
would pertain to their religious beliefs. The butchered and bloody animal, "opened," gutted, its internal organs, edible or not, removed, and
even some of the bones extracted, offered a rather unpleasant sight, so
that it may have been preferable to clean it up with a simple rinsing, repeated if necessary in clean, cool, water, before going any further. In the
"haute cuisine" of that land there was an interest, we believe, in at least
presenting a clean and irreproachable cut of meat to the source of heat.

Finally, we must keep in mind the method of cooking to be employed.
Most often, notably in B, it began in the kettle with browning, either dry or
with very little liquid. This stage left a residue both in the cooking vessel
and on the meat itself. This cooking method would draw juices from the
meat onto the bottom of the kettle, and the meat would be covered with
the same residue as the kettle, an undesirable "film" (šišītu) (Bi:65, iv:16
and 18) that had to be washed off, both from the meat and from the kettle.

These were the reasons for the baths, which either were simple rinsings or used "a lot of water" (this is how I interpret the expression, otherwise unknown, I believe, *mê maḫâsu*, literally "strike with water"), bringing to mind some kind of "purification" ritual, although Mesopotamian folklore, or religion, visible everywhere can hardly have had any meaning in such a purely technical context.

Cooking

The tablet that best illustrates this all-important moment is A, and it seems, in fact, to be completely devoted above all to it. Here again is an excerpt from this tablet, a reflection and summary of almost all the other recipes on it (A:55ff):

> **Salted broth.** Leg of mutton (?), but no other meat is used. Prepare water, add fat; dodder as desired, salt to taste; cypress; onion and *samidu;* cumin; coriander; leek and garlic, mashed with *kisimmu.* (Once it is cooked), it is ready to serve.

It is the same word for word throughout the recipes of the collection (except the one for *zamzaganu*, A:27ff, possibly transcribed from a separate culinary source). The procedure is simple: the cook was to prepare a "stock," and "cooking broth," in which (this is true for the "court bouillon" above) the meat would cook, assuming the complex taste and aroma of the broth itself and infusing its own flavor into it.

Once the choice of the main ingredient had been made (meat, and, from A:62, vegetables; even grain in Biv:34–50, etc.), water, the principal element, was first "put in place" (*kunnu*) in the cooking vessel. In the recipe for *zamzaganu* this is only assumed, as it was no doubt an obvious step.

First, "some fat" (*lipû*), mentioned throughout, was added. As explained by the Sumerian name for this substance, *ì-udu*, "sheep fat," the fat was taken preferably from the slaughtered animal—this is indicated more than once (but only in B and C, A doesn't enter into details)—and the cook was to "remove [*šalâpu*] the gristle [*širḫânu*]" that was usually on the fat and would have been difficult to chew (Bi:11, etc., and C:8). After the dish had been cooked, the liquid would be even more "fatty," and all the more appreciated, enriched with juices from the meat, and emitting the aroma from the multiple additions that had been made, either before or while cooking. This was called "pot fat" (Bi:18, etc.), or just "fat" (C:49, etc.), and it could be eaten immediately or used later as a culinary liquid, something we still practice today (Bi:18).

Here we put our finger on the exceptional advantages of "indirect cooking in liquid" and the enormous step forward that its discovery and generalized use had brought about in both the taste and the culinary arts of Mesopotamia. Demanding much less attention and surveillance than direct cooking, it also enhanced the flavor of the food being prepared, allowing unbounded richness and variety simply through the addition of a number of infinitely variable and combinable ingredients to the fatty water and the meat being cooked; and those ingredients, while cooking all together in the same broth, reinforced the liquid with their rich nutrition and flavor.

The recipe cited above calls for no fewer than ten additions. This is an unusual quantity but in no way exorbitant. If we look only at the recipes in A, such additions (most often the same ones) usually number four or five. But the flavoring ingredients in all of our recipes amount to the respectable number of thirty-six, which implies an amazing refinement of taste, and bespeaks an "haute" cuisine, an authentic gastronomy.

To better appreciate this refinement, let us review all these additions. We must first admit that a number of them are not truly identifiable: for the time being we cannot discern the exact meaning of the words that describe them—a serious disadvantage when (as in our case) we find ourselves in the presence of words which no living tradition, either directly or indirectly, no comparative reasoning, is able to recognize. The only exceptions are a few more frequently used terms that our lexicographers have been able to clarify more or less, with the understanding that we will never have precise definitions. So we have to supplement each "translation" with a question mark. A similar issue is that of weights and measures, where we are reduced to hypotheses or approximations. Ultimately we can derive only a rather vague idea of the true flavors resulting from the culinary labor.

Some of these ingredients (most of them botanical) appear to have been chosen to *add to the nutritional value of the dishes,* an essential concern in cooking, or at least to alter the food's consistency. This is the case with grain products, "breads," "cakes," or "mixtures," *bappiru, risnâtu,* as well as the *qalîtu* and *qaiiâtu* with a burned flavor, which further modified the flavor of the dish.

Another imposing category played a universal role in the nutritional realm as well as in the realm of flavor: the members of the onion family, for which those ancient gourmets, throughout their history and at least since the third millennium BCE, appear to have had an insatiable passion. Even the "indirect sources" contain evidence of this, and some facts

are surprising. Around the end of the third millennium, the daughter of
the king Su-Su'en was leaving for the land of Anšan with a few provisions
of butter, cheese, oil, and fruit, but we may wonder what she planned to
do with those "seven talents" (35 kg!) of garlic and a similar amount of
onions that she brought with her, if not to distribute them widely—no
doubt after having kept some for her own use.[66]

Our documents include at least five or six varieties; only three are
even slightly recognizable to us: the "onion" (*šusikillu*), the "leek" (*karšu*,
karašu), and "garlic" (*hazanu*), used whole or, more often, mashed or
chopped together, as we still do today to draw more flavor from them.
They were mixed with each other or with other ingredients. As for *samidu*,
šuhutinnû and *andahšu*, what exactly did they represent in this botanical
family?

According to the recipes, it would seem that those old gourmets had
discovered affinities, a complementarity of taste, among these plants,
which are, moreover, usually mentioned in couples (garlic and leek, notably); so they used them most often together, like our "fines herbes." Let
us recall here that there is no compelling evidence of a belief in a "supernatural," or "magical," or religious effect in the use of these or other ingredients: it was mainly, no doubt exclusively, a matter of taste.

Among additives to "broth," before or during cooking, sometimes at
the end and almost raw, some must have had the role of our spices,
which are more flavorful than nourishing and provide an enticing flavor
and aroma to the dish. The increasing number of them and the way they
are combined in dishes reveal the refined palates of those Mesopotamian
cooks and diners. One such plant, at least, appears to have given off a
particularly powerful aroma, since only "a few flowers"(?) (the text says
four) were needed for the entire dish to take on the name of the plant, but
we don't know what *halazzu* might have been (A: 52ff).

Other analogous, most often vegetal, products must have been included in the same category, apparently all native to the region (I know of
no imported products), most of which appear frequently in our sources,
both indirect and, more often, direct. We find them combined both in the
composition of *mersu*, and in "court bouillon."

There is "dodder"? (*kasû*); "mint"? (*ninû*); "cumin"? (*kamûnu, kamû*);
"dill"? (*šipittu*); "coriander"? (*kisibirru*); "arugula"? (*egengeru*); "cypress
cones"? (*šurmênu*); "rue"? (*sibburratu*); the enigmatic "wood" (*issû*), no
doubt aromatic; and one or two more, which we know nothing about,
such as *zurumu*.

A few milk products (*šizbu*) could also be used in the preparation of
dishes. Milk itself, sometimes mixed with water (A:20), or with butter-

milk (?) added (*itirtu*), could be used in kneading bread dough (Biv:*51*); butter (*ḫimêtu*) was always clarified in that warm land, that is, made out of boiled milk, and therefore did not become rancid; finally a few cheeses, all made out of curdled milk, were then dried and perhaps occasionally perfumed with herbs: is this *kisimmu*?

Sometimes fresh or almost fresh blood (*dâmu*) was added to broth, no doubt in small quantities. It was apparently taken from the slaughtered animal to be cooked, and was reserved for this purpose (A:*8, 14* etc.) We don't really know what flavor, or what likely nutritional advantage, was thought to be found in it. It was often blended with other ingredients (A:*43*; C*51*) to make a sort of "paste," as we call it, which was added to the broth and melted in it.

Beer (*šikaru*) was occasionally used as the liquid necessary for the preparation of a broth, thereby replacing water, at least in part (A:*62*; Biv:*7*). It was usually flavored by soaking some aromatic "wood" in it (Biv:*21*). This use of beer was rare, however.

Wine (*karânu*), which appeared later, and first from abroad, seems never to have found a culinary use; it is never mentioned in our recipes.

We do not know what *ṭâbâtu*, which we translate, for some unknown reason, as "vinegar," was made of; in itself, the word merely alludes to the "good flavor" of the product (from *ṭâbu*: good, pleasant). It almost certainly had nothing to do with true wine, as it does for us. It was used mainly, as we still use vinegar today, to sprinkle on meat before cooking, in order to firm and tighten it up before it is salted and sprinkled with mint (Biii:*43*). It was also used as a condiment for the cooked meat that was served separately from the broth, accompanied only by "greens" (Bii:*16*– *17*). It must have been rather strong, for at least once the cook was cautioned to "control its quantity carefully" (Biv:*21*). Was it derived from soured beer, or from some acidic syrup?

Honey (*dišpu*), which gave *mersu* its sweet taste, appears in our recipes only once, in Biv:*57*, for making a sort of "pancake" that was used as a holder for the meat.

Salt, whose specific designation, *ṭâbtu*, like that of vinagar, recalled the "good flavor" that it conferred, has already been mentioned. Here, and here alone, to my knowledge, it is in the plural form, *ṭâbâtu*—not to be confused with the name for vinegar. Before it was used it had to be "crushed" (*marâqu*) to be reduced to usable grains, for it was obtained in blocks (*kirbânu*). It is possible, although this is never explicitly said, that cooks used it quite systematically.

A liquid condiment, made not only of salt, but also of fish, shellfish, or grasshoppers more or less decomposed in brine, was called *siqqu*.It was not a seasoning, to be poured into broth to alter its flavor or consistency, but was an actual *food product*, one that was both nutritional and flavorful, used to enhance the taste of either cooked or raw food (most likely fish).

Regarding flavors and cuisine, we must remember that changes and fashions must have come into play, in Mesopotamia as everywhere else, changes that occurred from one land to another and from one era to another. Thus, in our three tablets we do not have the slightest mention of a famous condiment herb, *saḫlû* (from the Sumerian *za-ḫi-li*), a plant with a sharp taste (?), something like watercress (?), which was greatly enjoyed and widely used at certain times: it appears, for example, in the "court bouillon."

The use and the combination of these additional ingredients, of course, did not occur haphazardly: some were added at the beginning to the still cold water; others, as is suggested by the very ordering of the recipes, were added later, raw or barely cooked, perhaps even after cooking was completed. For example, in A:36, mashed *kisimmu* was added after the pot was taken off the heat. These nuances were all part of the "profession."

The recipes from tablet A, with the exception, perhaps, of that for *zamzaganu*, deal only with cooking in fatty broth. In almost all of them the main ingredient is meat. But the final four recipes demonstrate wonderfully that cooks also knew how to prepare vegetables in the same way, with meat (62–70) or without it (71ff). The vegetables therefore took on the rather rich flavor of the fatty broth, and when broken down or reduced to puree through cooking, they were softened and could be mashed and served as "porridges" (*šipku*: A:64), a pleasant and easy-to-eat variation, one that was apparently enjoyed.

Through their style, and in part their vocabulary, the recipes on B and C appear to be somewhat different (it would be interesting to make a close comparison of the recipe for francolins in A:58–61 and in Biv:1ff, and the recipe for *amursânu*-pigeon, in A:47–49 and Bi:50ff). But in spite of the smaller variety of additives, both tablets still involve cooking in fatty broth.

Not only were fleshy vegetables prepared in this way, as we just pointed out, but grain was also used, in the form of variously crushed seeds, as fine or coarsely ground flour. Cooked in fatty broth, the grain absorbed its flavor, turning into a hearty and tasty concoction similar to our semolina, polenta, or bulgur, which made a very good accompaniment to cooked meat; the Mesopotamians seem to have considered it delicious. C:18–43 presents an excellent recipe for this. The last recipe on

B (iv:42ff), the longest, has grouped together some half-dozen such dishes. Similarly, for the preparation of francolins, alone, the author gathered together at the beginning of the recipe, as if in a hurry, four or five procedures for fatty broth (Biv:3 – 18). Too stingy with indispensable stylistic specifications for our taste, at least for us foreigners, the entire passage and the recipe altogether are obscure and in places unclear. At least we can see that it still involves the same cooking method: in fatty broth.

Presentation of the Dish

Presentation was the third and final moment in culinary work: once the dish was cooked, it remained only to be served to those eating. According to the formula that is frequently, but irregularly, reiterated, it was "ready to serve" (A:39; 44, etc.; Bii:20; C:17), literally: "to present to the knife," which at that time was apparently the only utensil by means of which guests could dig into whatever they were eating so as to cut it up and put it in their mouths.

First of all, what exactly was eaten out of all that was cooked in the pot or kettle? Everything? That is, the meat with its accompaniments, as well as the broth? This is specified at least once (Bi:42ff):

> Just before serving, you take the platter prepared with a lining of crust, and you place the cooked birds on it carefully; you scatter the pluck and the cut-up gizzards that were (being cooked) in the pot over it, as well as the (little) *sebetu* rolls that were baked in the oven. You set aside the fatty broth in which the meat was cooked in the pot. You cover the serving dish with its pastry "cover" and bring it to the table.

Another indication in the same sense in Bii:15ff.

> When it is all cooked, I remove the pot from the fire, and before the broth cools [literally: "rested"], you rub the meat with garlic, add greens and vinegar. The broth may be eaten at a later time.

What was served was thus mainly meat and its accompaniment. It is possible that the broth was not normally served at the same time, as noted above; there was probably too much of it, and it was too thin to play the role of a reduced "sauce." The cooks do not seem to have thought up this latter type of culinary presentation, and the liquid part of the dish would have too easily overflowed its serving dish, or would have made the baked crust of its "false pie" too soggy. So they put the broth aside, either to serve it alone on another occasion or for other culinary uses. But to facilitate the consumption of the meat, which by itself may have been a bit dry, there was a pleasant and refreshing accompaniment: garlic, greens (green vegetables, probably raw, like our salads), and a liquid that was both aromatic and invigorating—"vinegar."

To honor and delight those eating—let us not forget that our recipes belong to a refined cuisine, for guests of a certain social caliber, and that we know nothing about the routine of ordinary meals without fanfare among simple folk—the chefs wanted to offer them the results of a truly elaborate culinary labor in all its glory, that is, a fully nourishing meal but also one most likely to charm the senses of sight and smell, as well as taste. Culinary aesthetics, affirmed and seen clearly in the "molds" of Mari, is still important to us today.

This is why the last part of some of our recipes—especially on B, more generous in this regard—are devoted to the supreme effort that was required of cooks in the *presentation of the dish*, the final arrangements to be given to the dish before it was served.

An initial sign of this concern appears, rather curiously, at the conclusion of the second recipe of B "an *amursânu*-pigeon" (Bi:50ff). A, which has a similar recipe (47–49), has no such ending. The passage on B is slightly deteriorated, and what it says is not completely clear, at least in the details. But it does appear that the effort of completion and of serving the dish revolved around two points.

First, the body of the animal, having been taken out of the broth, was placed on its serving shell of pastry. Then—and here the maneuver, if we understand it correctly, leaves us a bit perplexed—the legs were served: the thighs, the part considered the most flavorful, previously "roasted on the fire" and thus separate, were served apart from the body, which was covered in dough (*lišu*). The precise results escape us, but at least we see the double effort involved: to enhance (through bread dough) the nutritional value of the food, and to arrange the dish in an attractive way.

Again in B (i:17–47), which alone appears concerned with these questions of form, the end of the first recipe ("small birds") is devoted to what I call "presentation in a false pie." The author explains at length how to knead and prepare three types of bread dough, slightly different in ingredients and in flavor. They will be used to create the "false pie," composed of a serving shell on which the cooked birds will be "arranged in good order" (*sadâru:* one might understand: "tastefully," "artistically"), along with the chopped up pieces of pluck and gizzard, and the little *sebutu* rolls all placed on top and all around; all of this to be covered with the other shell in the guise of a "cover," but obviously not fused to the bottom part. Here, let us repeat, we have a desire both to enrich the dish nutritionally as much as possible and to attract attention to it: to pique the guests' interest and appetites at the sight of such an enticing culinary construction.

The third recipe (Bii:*39ff*) proceeds in approximately the same way. Only the "cover" appears to be missing. It would, moreover, hardly fit over the entire cooked bird resting on its "shell." But the cook still strives to embellish the bird: it is served on the "platter" (the passage, rather mutilated, retains its secrets) in a single piece, both the thighs and the neck tied together (*patâlu*) against the sides, as we still do today. The rest is damaged after *48*, but the lingering mention of "grilled barley" (*qalîtu*), would suggest that the entire dish was accompanied by a porridge of roasted barley. We are far from sure, but given what follows, and in particular the last recipe of B (below), it is at least likely.

These steps are again employed in the course of the last recipe, which is long and obscure, of B (iv:*1–end*). In it we find—if I am not mistaken—in iv:*32* the kneading of a shell, along the lines of i:*17ff*, that was also to be used as a serving dish. Farther along (iv;*51ff*), and, it must be said, without anything but "culinary logic" to suggest the connection I am establishing here, we also find the kneading of another, rather different dough, which could serve as a "cover." As in i:*35ff*, to "keep it pliable" it was necessary to put some "oil" on it after it was baked.

Owing in part to the poor condition of the tablet, in part to the taciturnity of the author, who in addressing the cooks of his own time and country could be content simply to suggest rather than to explain, we do not possess, or do not understand, the subtleties of the recipe. But what we can imagine or reconstruct from these fragments gives us the idea of a dish that was well conceived, lavish, and complex in its presentation. It would have included a bottom shell of pastry functioning as an edible platter, and on top (or perhaps on the side, but this is not said) a porridge, if desired, from among the list drawn up in iv:*32–49*, and perhaps also, unless this is again a tacit variant, a curious mixture of mashed members of the onion family, with honey and butter (iv:*55ff*), on which the francolins were placed, sheltered by a "cover." If the last four or five lines were legible or decipherable, this culinary enigma might be solved. What remains of it and what we believe we understand evokes something that is both hazy and vast, yet corresponds with the presentation, more than once made explicit, of a sumptuous, refined, if not pretentious dish, in perfect accord with that elaborate, demanding, lavish, and often tortuous cuisine suitable for a civilization that could afford it.

COOKS AND CULINARY
TRADITION

Let us look separately at those Mesopotamians who were isolated, who did not live at home—shepherds and agricultural workers, far from home, in their fields or their grazing lands; solitary travelers or nomads; soldiers at war—whose interest in food represented the baseline of cuisine, food preparation with minimal fuss. With very little effort they could prepare, right on the fire, a meal that was quite simple but nourishing. To fill in their silence, and since in this domain things probably haven't changed much since those distant times, we can imagine them through the culinary behavior of the nomadic Bedouins, as they were observed only a century ago by Fr. P. Jaussen:[67]

> Having scarcely dismounted, the Arab pours a little water from his flask into a wooden vessel, adds a little flour that he carries in a leather pouch, and begins to knead; he adds a little salt when he has some, which is a rare exception. During that time, his companion has gathered some wood, or dried grass, or dung, and has lit a fire. The fire, mixed with a lot of ash, is ready as soon as the improvising baker has finished kneading his handful of flour. The dough, sprinkled with flour and pounded well, is shaped into a round disk and placed in the middle of the fire, from which a little ash and burning wood has previously been removed; the bread is then covered completely. Thirty minutes pass: using a firebrand the Arab removes the ashes and the coals that cover the dough and turns it over; otherwise it would be burned and charred on top and completely uncooked on the bottom. The bread is flipped over in this way two or three times until it is judged to be ready: it is taken out of the fire and eaten warm.

Can one imagine any greater frugality? That must have ordinarily been the lot of many people, and for numerous reasons. Some were probably used to the meal and may even have derived some pleasure from it. We have already referred to a passage from the *Poem of Erra*, whose author, through the mouths of professional soldiers, celebrates the ascetic and exalting life of the old guard. Here is the entire passage:

I/51 **For real men, going off to war,**
      It's a feast! . . .
57   **The best bread from the city**
      Cannot match the loaf under ashes!
      The sweetest beer
      Cannot match the water from a flask!

Cooking at Home

But those were extreme, if not exceptional, conditions, and things were quite different, not nearly as plain, for the majority of the population, who lived in villages and towns "at home" with their families.

In the realm of food, hence in the culinary realm, the most important person was necessarily the wife, the mother—the "housewife," as she might be called. This was true practically everywhere.[68]

Consequently, although the husband could, if he wished, leave home for a time, provided he left enough food for the family ("*Code of Hammurabi*, §133ff),[69] since it was normally he who provided a living for his family, a wife's absence was viewed with great disapproval, and she would be considered, as is expressed in the same "Code" (§142), a *partyer*, a "loose woman." Her principal role was with her family "at home," where, in order not to risk damaging the cohesion and the unity of the family, or even to give rise to suspicions or nasty rumors, which would cause her to be "pointed at" (§152) for having "defied" her husband" (§143), she was to devote herself above all to household duties, not only to raising the children and maintaining the home but also to preparing the indispensable daily meals for everyone in her family. As a Sumerian proverb says:[70]

> When (the mistress) left the house and entered the streets, the slave girl, in the absence of her mistress, made her own banquet.

In other words: it is chaos!

In the *Epic of Gilgameš* (VI:70), when the hero returns triumphant from the Cedar Forest, his strength, his verve, and his prestige attract the attention of the goddess Ištar, always on the lookout for handsome males, who crudely invites him into her bed. But on guard and suspicious, Gilgameš refuses, scornfully reminding her of the names and lamentable stories of her multiple lovers, whom she had seduced and then dropped. The last among them, he reminds her, a gardener, had at first escaped her clutches through candor or shrewdness; he had not understood, or had not tried to understand, what she expected of him, which was proposed in truly lascivious terms. He had understood, or pretended to understand, her proposal in terms of food, not sex. Speaking of food, he immediately refers to his mother, the uncontested ruler in that domain (VI:71):

> Me? What is it you want from me?
> Has my mother not baked, and have I not eaten
> that I should now eat food under contempt and curses.

Although we lack specific details, cooking and all the daily culinary work in Mesopotamia was thus usually the domain of the "housewife," who was celebrated for that role.

There is a small literary piece, bilingual, quite brief, and rather obscure, most likely from the second millennium BCE, in which, in an edifying and moralizing (?) passage the author apparently wanted to draw a contrast between the irreproachable wife, devoted to her domestic duties, and the lazy woman, disorganized and good for nothing. And what inspires praise for the former?[71]

1   The house where beer is never lacking:
    She is there!
2   The house rich in soup:
    That is her place!
3   The house where there is bread in abundance:
    She is the one who cooks it!

Lacking true primary sources, we can, however, find indirect but rather moving traces of a wife's housekeeping and culinary vocation, notably in a few surviving marriage contracts that record the bride's dowry: the goods that were handed down to her by her family and that she would take with her when she left—theoretically for good—her paternal home, where she had been born and had always lived up until her marriage, to "enter her husband's home" as a "legitimate wife," normally without returning. To me there is always something sad and touching in these documents, both from the perspective, perhaps old-fashioned, of a young woman's final departure, and from reading the often modest, but significant, list of goods that the emigrant was going "to take with her." Sometimes there were small parcels of land, even a "servant girl," but there were also worn garments and simple utensils, which suggested the trappings of everyday life. Here is one such example:[72]

1   A servant girl, by the name of Tarâm-Akkad;
    [Such] clothes, other than those she is wearing;
    Two (?) hoods, plus the one on her head;
    A grinder for fine flour;
5   A semolina grinder;
    A mortar, in stone;
    Two vessels filled with oil;
    Two "beds,"
    Two chairs;
10 A pillow;
    Two large spoons;
    Three small spoons.
    These are the goods that were given to Damiqtu, *šugîtu*-priestess,
15 Daughter of Ilima-ahi, by her father and mother,
    When they married her to [literally: introduced into the home of]
    Sîn-išme anni, the son of Tarîbu.

Aside from the furniture and the personal clothing, there is an immediate reference here (other contracts are even more prolific and picturesque) to the young wife's future as a housewife, indeed as a cook.

Official Cuisine

In ancient Mesopotamia, as elsewhere, beyond the daily and little-known needs of the simple subjects living at home, there was also what might be called an haute cuisine, an official cuisine, the operators and practitioners of which, almost always men because there was something "learned," something regimented and complicated, about this kind of cooking, were evidently skilled practitioners, professionals.

In Akkadian they were called *nuḫatimmu*, a term borrowed, no doubt along with the technique to which it referred, from the Sumerians, who called them *muḫaldim* (regularly abbreviated to *mu*), whose basic meaning escapes us.

That word, common and used extensively, had enough synonyms and equivalents, or quasi equivalents (we are not always in a position to judge), to reflect the wealth of culinary techniques. They may have been archaic terms that fell out of common use: such as *engû* or *endibbu*, curiosities about which we know nothing else, or paraculinary professions, the exact details of which escape us; the *luraqqu/lurakku* in Mari, at least in the first third of the second millennium BCE, seems to have specialized in the production of sauces and condiments such as *siqqu*.

Around the *nuḫatimmu* were other professionals who, each in his own line of work, must have practiced various techniques and assured various stages in the preparation of dishes: the *êpišânu* ("preparers") and the *mubannû* ("embellishers"), perhaps devoted (and we know there was a reason for this) to the nutritional and "artistic" *presentation* of the dishes. The *êpû* (let's call them "bakers") were responsible mainly for bread, the omnipresent and multiform food. Others were devoted to "sweets" (*kakardinnu/karkadinnu*), "pastry chefs," if you will; the creator of the *mersu* cake in Mari may have been one of these. Working outside the kitchen were those who contributed to the preparation of the very rich and varied culinary ingredients: millers, dairy farmers, butchers, and the like, all of whom were professionals, each in charge of his own domain. It goes without saying that their task could be carried out, if needed, by the cooks themselves; in our recipes, although this is not mentioned in connection with large livestock or game, the cook himself slaughtered and dressed the birds to be cooked.

Centered around the cook and directed by him, that auxiliary group seems to have constituted, at least on occasion, a type of "brigade" in the preparation of official or liturgical banquets at the palace or temple.

Like all professions whose function was of some importance, that of the *nuḫatimmu* was quite far-reaching and absorbing—as we have already glimpsed—inasmuch as its success depended greatly on the tastes of others. Thus a more complete, lengthy, and serious initiation was required than for professions that were less encyclopedic and more easily learned. In that land, especially, where there was never much concern with theoretical "principles," which as such were yet inaccessible to them, instruction, especially in cooking, could only be dispensed on a "casuistic" level of know-how: through practical exercise, on a case-by-case basis that demanded prolonged contact with one or more experts in the field, one or more qualified "masters." By watching the chef work and by helping him day by day, the disciple learned to imitate him, all his gestures and tricks, all the reactions required by the infinite challenges of food preparation.

Luckily we possess an illustration of this in a small number of contracts for an apprenticeship in the profession of *nuḫatimmu*. Here is one, which must date from around 550 BCE:[73]

(The present document testifies) that Ina-qâti-Nabû-balṭu, in the service of Itti-Marduk-balâṭu since the month of Ab [this was the fifth month of a twelve-month year] of the sixth year of Cyrus, king of Babylon and of the World, until the next month of Araḫsammu [the eighth], will remain with Riḫeti, server of Basis, in order to learn, completely, the profession of cook.

In this case, the apprenticeship covered around fifteen months, and to judge from what we know and can guess, that much time was indeed needed to acquire the know-how and practice that such a complex and demanding discipline required.

This is even more true since practitioners exerted considerable technical authority in their domain. Constantly "in front of his stoves," the cook had to confront situations that were often unexpected or delicate, on which the success of his work depended. And the recipes, as we immediately noted, simply trace the outline of the procedure, rarely delving into details.

For example, they never precisely indicate the *time* or the *duration* of the procedures; it was up to the cook to decide those according to the concrete facts of a situation, which he could not know until preparation had begun—until he had the menu and the ingredients to be used on a specific occasion. In the recipe for "court bouillon," it is merely indicated that the cook begins with a pot filled with six liters of water and must let it boil until it is reduced to roughly one liter, volumes that were obviously measured by sight.

Nor is *quantitative information* provided. When a number appears in the course of the recipes, it never indicates a quantity strictly speaking, but only an order of magnitude. In Bi:16, in which the cook is told to add certain other members of the onion family and "ten scoops of cool water" to the broth as it begins to heat up, the ten scoops obviously don't imply exactly fifteen centiliters but simply a "small quantity." The "four blades (?)" of *ḫalazzu*, to be tossed into the broth of A:53 to give it its aroma and flavor are simply "a few" flowers (?); and so on.

On this same subject, we constantly encounter deliberately vague phrases that suggest the amount and the proportion of various additives: salt "depending on the grain" (A:12; 29; etc.)—in other words, what the cook in that instance would have judged sufficient to be reduced into usable powder; or dodder "as desired" (A:34); "enough" water (Bii:4); and so forth.

Only the chef could determine how to proceed: following a recipe, he had "full power" to make decisions based on the dish he was preparing, the number of guests anticipated, and other unique and specific data. He would make those last-minute, impromptu decisions on which success depended, requiring sure and rapid judgment as well as a great deal of professional experience.

In the apprenticeship contract just mentioned, the person concerned, Ina-qâti-Nabû-balṭu, was thus "in service" in the household of Itti-Marduk-balâṭu, who had placed him in apprenticeship, and his "initia-

tor," Riḫeti, was similarly "in the service of" Basis. In other words, although some cooks (I have no evidence for this) were able to practice
"freelance," cooks overwhelmingly exercised a "servile" profession: in
the house of and at the expense of some high-ranking person who was
rich enough to hire one or several of those specialists in "haute cuisine,"
or "official cuisine," qualified to prepare banquets in their "employer's"
home.

But it was an honorable occupation and carried prestige. Its representatives who were connected to a temple even had the honor of being
declared "priests" of that temple (šangû), an honorific title if ever there
was one. The authors of the great "List of Gods" (An-Anum), wishing to
draw up a coherent "theological" tableau of the divine crowd, chose to
take the least prestigious among them and to make them members of the
houses of the greater: in doing so they selected the professions of "seat-
bearer," "gardener," "lieutenant," and also "cook" as always respectable,
thereby highlighting the dignity of the culinary profession. One god is
thus named "Cook of Marduk," and another "Cupbearer" (An-Anum, II,
263ff). Among mortals as among the gods, however, it was well understood that the only people who could employ cooks and offer them normal work conditions, adequate kitchens and equipment, as well as the
occasions to exercise their talent and to organize "great meals" and
"banquets," in short, that "official" or "haute" cuisine truly worthy of the
efforts of the cooks, were the great of this world: not only the priests who
ministered to the gods, and the king and his family in their palace, but
what we may well call the "upper class."

To serve the members of that stratum in terms of their resources,
their desire for ostentation and magnificence, a rather large number of
cooks was sometimes required to meet their needs, so that kitchens and
equipment must often have been vast and complex.

Toward the end of the Neo-Assyrian Period, in the eighth to the seventh centuries, we are informed that in Nineveh, the "House of the
Queen" alone included[74]

300 various domestic servants
300 launderers
220 cupbearers
400 cooks
400 "pastry chefs"
200 scribes

A comparison of the numbers speaks volumes!

Without sufficient documentation, it is not easy to describe these cooks in their everyday working world. We can at least imagine them through a few isolated texts. For example, in an official document that ratified a pious food foundation of the Assyrian king Tukulti-Ninurta I (1244–1208 BCE) in honor of the goddess Šarrat-nipḫa, reference is made to the cooks employed there, whose daily routine consisted of:[75]

Cutting the wood to be burned,
Cleaning the pots,
Filling them with water.
Lighting the wood, from below,
And thereby preparing the meals.

And the author of *The Adapa Story*,[76] from the middle of the second millennium, presents his hero, a "cook" in the temple of Enki/Ea, in Eridu, as follows:

Pure, clean of hands, anointed one
 who was solicitous after divine rites,
He performed the baker's office with the baker,
He performed the baker's office with the bakers of Eridu,
Every day he (himself) made the food and drink for Eridu('s cult).
He prepared the table with his own clean hands,
Nor without him was the table cleared.

And this is why, to fulfill his professional duties and to stock the temple, notably with fish (Eridu was located near the Persian Gulf), Adapa goes fishing every day, where the adventure recounted in his "legend" awaits him.

Culinary Tradition

These multitudes of cooks took over from each other in successive generations throughout the multimillennial history of ancient Mesopotamia, constantly enriching and improving their techniques through their cumulative and selective work, so that the techniques themselves became integrated into their way of life, thus giving further value to that noble civilization.

The Epic of Gilgameš, while describing the Flood, indirectly emphasizes the zeal with which the ancient Mesopotamians preserved the accomplishments of their culture: the hero of the disaster, Utanapištim ("*I-have-found-life*"), as he is called, is instructed by Ea to include the *craftsmen* on his life-saving boat, along with the members of his family and the animals necessary to resupply the fauna. According to another tradition, adopted and propagated by Berossus, a priest and scholar from

Babylon who, around 300 BCE, published in Greek the traditions and history of his land:

> Kronos [which is what he calls Ea, through syncretism][78] commanded Sisithros [the Greek rendering of the other name of the same hero: Ziud-sud-ra; in Sumerian: "Life of prolonged days"] to put in a safe place all that was written in the city of Šippar.[79]

These people were therefore not only conscious of their high and original culture but were anxious to preserve as much as possible of what they had accomplished: on the one hand—the oldest method—through living memory and its usual depository, *oral tradition*, the principal holders of which were the storytellers with their "secrets"; on the other, through the use of *writing*, invented around the end of the fourth millennium and practiced at an increasing rate. Writing set down forever the thoughts, the knowledge, and the know-how of the ancient Mesopotamians, making them concrete and solidifying them, while ensuring them unlimited survival in both time and space. It is clear that the Yale Culinary Tablets were a part of this written culinary tradition, the flotsam and jetsam of an enormous shipwreck. By putting them down in writing, the Mesopotamians wished only and primarily to *preserve* the secrets of their culinary techniques, but *not to disseminate* them, as we do when we publish cookbooks. In a land where hardly anyone knew how to read or write, such a goal would have been in vain. At the very least, these tablets would have provided a crutch if something had been forgotten.

From what was probably a torrent of written culinary tradition, all we have left, besides the remains of the "court bouillon" and, in a sense, of the *mersu*, are the three tablets that are the subject of the present work. They constitute a kind of snapshot, taken at a given point and a given moment in an endless sequence. As to what came after or went before, we currently possess nothing else relating even to the "haute cuisine" described in our tablets, much less of the details of that basic, universal, yet unknown "household cuisine." Aside from the tablets, we are left in total darkness. We can only indulge in conjectures, which suggest that the cuisine of Mesopotamia was "transmitted" with a few major elements of its civilization to neighboring peoples, and passed on, from them to still others, in the march of the centuries—a history that is inaccessible to us. We might imagine that the cooks of that ancient land could have left something substantial to other cuisines around them: the use of the *tinûru*, for example, and of unleavened bread in round, flat loaves, as well as their passion not only for the redoubtable onion family but for multiple condiments and seasonings, and even the custom of serving meat accompanied and surrounded by a layer of unleavened bread or enclosed in a "false pie shell." But we are not able to continue much farther on such a dark path scattered with pitfalls.

For a cautious historian, the essential fact—even if there remain only occasional fragments—is that the ancient Mesopotamians, at a moment and in circumstances about which we know nothing, wrote down technical formulas, and specifically, among others, those dealing with the local cuisine.

We will never know how the scribes obtained the contents of the documents. From the mouth of some expert, in dictation? The oral style is obvious. Or perhaps the expert himself may spontaneously have begun to write or dictate what he knew—like a wise old man wanting to pass on his vast experience to his son.

One thing is certain—and it is not at all surprising among these great classifiers and determined list makers—the inscribed recipes were all *arranged* and not thrown willy-nilly onto their clay foundation. Among the thousands of documents unearthed, we have also recovered a number of other recipes, notably medical, for medicines and various therapies, along with instructions. They were similarly distributed in large collections, from which the practitioners, who had to be literate and thus capable of understanding what they were reading, could choose information by virtue of multiple criteria, and apply it on the spot.

Tablet C is not at issue here; it is not a "collection," since the three recipes inscribed on it are obviously unrelated—a meat dish; a grain porridge dish; another meat dish. Rather, it looks like a meal plan. On the other hand, the choice and the ordering of the recipes on tablets A and B strike the reader immediately—proof of their abundance and the wealth of the local cuisine.

For A, what is initially significant is the "total" at the end, which sums up the contents exactly (77ff) and therefore explains the meaning of the arrangement:

(That is) twenty-one meat broths
(and) four vegetable broths

There are, in all, twenty-five recipes, and they are put in order, even if that order is less rigorous than *our* logic might wish. Meat presides over all (1–61); then vegetable elements are added (62–70); and, at the end, meat disappears in favor of vegetables (71ff). The first recipe (1ff) appears to have been chosen as the most elementary and exemplary. The others become gradually more diverse and more complex, making use of just about the entire menagerie of animals available to them for their

defining ingredient: first the large wild four-footed animals, deer (*11*ff)
and gazelle (*15*); then domestic animals; kid (*17*), after which one ex-
pects to see lamb, which appears farther on (*31*), and ram (*33*). It is possible that among these recipes—why? how? through what steps?—
others were interspersed by virtue of criteria or circumstances about
which we know nothing, for the meaning of all the "titles" is often difficult
to interpret. After *47*, at least—and perhaps already at *37* with that enigmatic *bidšud*, even with the *zamzaganu* of *26*, birds begin to appear (pigeons in *47*; and "francolins" in *58*). Concerning "leg of mutton" (?) (*50*),
and with the exception of the one that immediately follows, which was
interpolated (*52*), a certain number of recipes arise that seem to require
all sorts of meat. Anyone undertaking a cursory reading of A cannot deny
that the original collection *may have been* more systematic, and that a
more obvious order was destroyed by the displacement and insertion of
recipes almost at random—which implies an entire literary history! It is
therefore possible that, constructed as it is and rather far from the general scheme of all the others, the recipe for *zamzaganu* (*26*ff) was borrowed from another culinary tradition and inserted here. Indeed, at least
two recipes that were introduced into A were taken from completely different cultural milieus: the "Assyrian" one of *3*ff, from the north, and,
more particularly, the "Elamite" one (*45*ff), from the southeast, whose
original name was even preserved and cited, as if to better emphasize its
foreign nature—an interesting phenomenon, since it indicates that cultural exchanges even involved food and drink (which is confirmed by the
example of wine, below).

That said, what becomes apparent throughout the twenty-five recipes of A, which convey the general line of Mesopotamian cuisine, are the
generous seasonings, the number and variety of its seasoning products
and "spices," and the tablet's complete absence of serious concern with
"aesthetics," the refinement and presentation of the dishes.

With regard to this terseness, reminiscent of the style of "culinary
guides" such as Escoffier's, which are meant primarily for professionals,
B strikes us by its detail and chattiness. Its style is not at all "telegraphic"
but flowing, and its instructions are complete: unlike A, it is not content
simply to sketch the steps that mark the main stages in a recipe. Whereas
A neglects detail, B leaves nothing in the dark (especially in its first three
recipes) about the physical, even anatomical preparation of the animal
before it is cooked. B too recommends "fatty broth," though the list of its
ingredients and additions is more modest. There are some that it ignores,
or never uses—such as dodder, cumin, cypress; and certain grain mixtures such as *bappiru* and *risnâtu*—but it does include other ingredients

such as "vinegar," "aromatic wood," and rue. And, as we have stressed, it emphasizes "presentation." What it describes, as compared with A, is certainly part of the same "family" of cuisine, but it seems to represent a different "school": it is the only one to insist on a certain number of cooking procedures that are absent on A—precooking and browning, as well as washings of both the meat and the kettle. On these points, one might say that the two collections, A and B, are complementary to each other, each developing in its own way the same culinary techniques, but describing them differently.

This distinction can be better illustrated if we indulge in a painstaking comparison of at least the two recipes that are found on both A and B; the ones for *amursânu*-pigeon (A:47ff, and Bi:50ff) and "francolins" (A:58–61 and Biv:1ff).

B is the only tablet, incidentally, to list multiple recipes within a single culinary instance or, when describing one recipe, to refer to another (iii:38):

> To prepare *kippu*-birds in broth, it should be prepared the same as for [detailed above] *agarukku-birds*.

And again, a bit farther on, the gaps in the tablet prevent us from knowing in detail what was necessary, and how, to reuse one for the other (iii:49):

> To prepare *kamkam*-birds in broth, it should be prepared like that [explained above] of *agarukku*-birds.

Tablet B accumulates recipes, like *variants* within a single recipe. Its seventh (all of iv) does this the most, which muddies the waters since it neglects to point out that it is going from one variant to another, or is content with a short "or" (*šaniš*, in iv:10, and perhaps 16). There are five such examples in iv:6–18; and six in iv:34–38.

Nor must we forget those two excerpts that include the curious alternation of the "teaching style," the "I" of the master who knows and wants to instill what he is doing as an example, and the "you" of the disciple when the master is directly addressing him and explaining to him what he must do. Here we even discover something about the manuscript translation that must have come *before* the present appearance of B: in order to explain this strange style there must have been at least two renderings of the text of that tablet, one using the "you" and the other the "I," from which a copyist, for a reason that escapes us, derived the text that we have before us, incorporating that stylistic amalgam to the strangest effect.

DRINKS

Perhaps even more than eating, drinking is one of our constant and essential needs. Yet although we find frequent evidence in our archives, either directly or through allusion, of what was drunk, we are far from learning as much on that subject as about what was eaten. No doubt this realm either was less complicated or involved less innovative imagination.

There were two large categories of beverages: "natural" ones, which required no preparation, or hardly any, and the more elaborate "fermented" drinks.

"Natural" Beverages

Water

In such a flat landscape with hardly any hills, especially in its southern part, there were practically no sources of fresh water. But under the earth was an immense phreatic layer, which mythologically was imagined to be coextensive with the territory of humankind and was believed to be the realm of the great god Enki/Ea. Drawn from the river or from a canal, but most often from wells, water (*mû*), indispensable for life and for many other things, was almost everywhere and at all times the first universal drink, provided that it was "clear" (*zakû*) and "cool" (*kaṣû*). People regularly kept a stock of it in their homes, in the coolest part of the house, in large porous vessels where it was rid of its potential deposits, and remained cold. When transported, it was usually carried in leather flasks (*nâdu*).

"To drink" was written ideographically somewhat like "to eat": instead of the pictogram of "bread" being inserted into that of "mouth," signifying "to eat," the pictogram of "water" was inserted into that of "mouth."[80] And one of the common practices for referring to sustenance in general—"food and drink"—made use of the same universal binomial: "bread and water." Thus a medical text, to announce an improvement in the condition of a patient who could no longer consume anything promises that

> he is going to experience a remission and will once again begin to feed himself [literally: "eat bread and drink water"].[81]

It is possible that, whether by preference or out of necessity and aside from its essential role in preparing broths, water alone was ordinarily consumed at the meals of the more humble of the population, or by those who could not afford other drinks, as could the wealthy.

All the same, despite the skimpiness or absence of information on this point, it is not unreasonable to presume that in a culture so refined in matters of taste—a fact of which we should be convinced by now—people sought, and easily found, something to add to water (insipid by itself, after all) so as to derive pleasure from drinking it, something to add an agreeable, sweet, or aromatic flavor. This could have been done through "infusions" or "decoctions," familiar to doctors who prescribed them through their potions and medicines. Even today, in Iraq and in the surrounding area, dried lemons, crushed and boiled (šai nûmi Basrâ; lemûn šai), constitute a pleasant and refined beverage, drunk hot or cold. Every culture has its tea.

To avoid plain water, commonplace and perhaps even depressing, the Mesopotamians may have doctored it with fruit juice, easily extracted from pomegranates, grapes, and other fruits; or they may have drunk those juices neat. Preparation was done on demand, since the product could not be preserved. As far as we know, there was never a juice-making "industry," such as existed for fermented beverages.

Milk

In that land of extensive livestock-raising, milk held a separate place in the realm of food: it was both a food because of its nutritional value, and a beverage because of its liquidity and flavor; so we find it grammatically ordered both by the verb "to eat" (akâlu), and that of "to drink" (šatû). However, it could only be preserved a few hours in its natural state; it "turned" very quickly. Thus it was often transformed into derivative products that played an important role in the local diet: cream, buttermilk, butter, and various cheeses. We have already pointed out how those products were used in Mesopotamian cuisine. Only a character such as Enkidu, in his still "wild" state, could "have had the habit of suckling only the milk of beasts;" and only those who raised animals, who lived alongside their herds, were ordinarily in a position to enjoy fresh milk in its primary liquid state. For the general population it could scarcely be counted as a regular drink.

It is possible, though we have no evidence, that curdled milk was used to make what in Iraq is now called *laban*. When whipped with cool water it makes *šenîna*, a refreshing beverage.

Apart from shepherds or dairy professionals, however, we have evidence that milk could be drunk as a luxury beverage. In a ritual of the temple of Anu in Uruk found on a tablet (which we will cite at greater length below) from a few centuries before the common era, this is how the drinks found on the divine table are listed:

> Each day, throughout the year, for the large morning meal, you will place on the Table of Anu . . . 18 golden pitchers, 7 to the right—that is, 3 filled with "barley beer;" and 4 with *labku*-beer; and 7 to the left—that is, 3 with "barley beer;" and 2 with *labku*-beer; 1 with *nâšu* beer; and 1 with *zarbaba* beer, as well as milk, in an alabaster pitcher.[82]

The same procedure was followed for the "small morning meal," and the "large and small afternoon meals." But for the last two meals milk was not to be served.

This omission in the afternoon can be explained: milking was done in the morning, and after a few hours milk was not in a condition to be served. Other analogous rituals also mention milk, sometimes even "sugared" (*matqu*). It was thus indeed a drink, but it was a luxury beverage, and except for shepherds and livestock-raisers and their neighbors it was reserved for the gods, or for the great of the world.

Fermented Beverages

We have found no reference to *lactic* fermentation used to create drinks such as the Caucasian *kephyr* or the *koumys* of the nomads of central Asia. To our knowledge the only type of fermentation used in Mesopotamia was the *alcoholic* fermentation of malt to produce beer and of the grape to produce wine.

Beer

In Mesopotamia since the earliest of times, the omnipresent grain crops provided not only the very foundation of the Mesopotamians' diet—bread—but also their principal beverage, which was beer.

The ideogram for beer, a significant presence that already appears in the earliest documents of cuneiform writing, from around the end of the fourth millennium BCE, represents a large vessel filled with water and grain—highly evocative of the brewery! ▷ It corresponded to the Sumerian kaš, the name for beer in that language. We don't know the original meaning of that word, which may have been borrowed from a different people (we have no idea which); almost none of the Sumerian vocabulary for the manufacture of beer seems indigenous to the Sumerian language. The technique for making beer must therefore have come from elsewhere. In Akkadian, the principal term, of Semitic origin, used to designate beer was šikaru, which signified "intoxicating liquid," thus named, it would seem, for its surprising ability to cast the body and the mind into an altered, somewhat beatific state, which rendered the beverage all the more enjoyable. Incidentally, the ancient Mesopotamians do not seem to have abused the drink: cases of drunkenness appear to have been rare, judging from our sources, which, of course, don't tell us everything!

Ever since the time of these first graphic traces in the "archaic tablets from Uruk" or even earlier, beer continued to reign unchallenged over the local culture until the end of the first millennium BCE, and even into the common era, in numerous presentations, names, and flavors, but obviously far from what we think of as beer. Although necessarily different from our beer, it was still essentially made from a base of various grains, first germinated and malted in damp conditions and then, once malting was completed, heated in water into which various aromatic products had been added. (Hops were unknown in that area, but dodder was used, and many other flavoring agents, as well). Then the mash was left to ferment.

For an introduction to this beverage—without claiming to present it in all its infinite, fastidious, and, from our perspective, often unimaginable details—we may turn to a selection from a Sumerian text from the turn of the third millennium, discovered and excellently translated by Miguel Civil. It is a rather short poem in two parts that were originally independent; the second, some thirty lines long, is what we would call a "drinking song," the only one known so far, I believe, in the literature of that land, whose tone and enthusiasm indicate how beer has inspired so much passion and good cheer through the millennia, much as wine does in France:

49   The gakkul [beer] vat, the gakkul vat, . . .
      The gakkul vat, which makes the liver happy,
      The lam-sá-re vat, which rejoices the heart!
      The ugur-bal jar, a fitting thing in the house,

The šá-gub jar, which is filled with beer! (. . .)

57 The beautiful vessels, are ready on (their) *potstands!* . . .

What makes your heart feel wonderful,

Makes (also) our heart feel wonderful.

Our liver is happy, our heart is joyful (. . .)

70 I will make cupbearers, boys, (and) brewers stand by,

While I turn around the abundance of beer,

Drinking beer, in a blissful mood, Drinking *liquor,* feeling exhilarated

75 With joy in the heart (and) a happy liver.[83]

This remarkable infatuation with that beatific liquid is translated in a different way in the other part of the poem (the first forty-eight lines). Beer is celebrated there purely and simply for its ontological value and its supernatural powers: it is divinized, placed in the ranks of the gods, even if it has never occupied a very high place there.

On this supernatural plane it bore the transparent Sumerian name of *Nin-ka-si:* "the Lady who fills the mouth," daughter of Enlil and of Ninhursag, his wife. In Akkadian it was called *Siriš,* or *Siris,* a Semitic term that refers to fermentation.[84] This goddess was believed to accomplish by herself, both as prototype and model, all the procedures of the brewery. There is no need to detail those procedures here.

Except for a mutilated text from the beginning of the second millennium BCE, we have not yet recovered a "recipe" for beer, one that is true and complete, although there is every reason to believe that more than one existed, whether written down or not. After two or three millennia, at the least, they would be fairly obscure.

It suffices for the time being to have learned that beer, through its existence, its consolations, and its delights, might have offered the ancient Mesopotamian population, beginning in the most distant times, a kind of gustative ideal, a source of pure pleasure, one within the reach of (almost) everyone, and good for counterbalancing many of the worries of existence. This was true of beer perhaps to an even greater extent than the delights of the table, which were less accessible, more refined, and, moreover, in their highest and most succulent state, not for the common man. In a word, to cite a Sumerian proverb;[85]

the pleasure—it is the beer! The discomfort—it is the journey!

In the passage cited above concerning the ritual of the temple of Anu, at Uruk, we find the names of several varieties of beer in their original forms, still untranslatable.

On this subject, it is better to call upon the subtleties and intricacies of our own wine lists to acknowledge, at least, the diversity and the wealth of the varieties of Babylonian beer and the vocabulary associated with it.

The second-to-last tablet of the "Great Encyclopedia," in the chapter on food,[86] despite its many gaps gives a good idea of that abundance. There were beers "of nice appearance," "of good quality," of "superior quality," or "prime," but also "inferior" beers. There were some "of the year" or "old" (but not necessarily better, and perhaps "turned"). There were "sweet beers," even "very sweet" ones. There were those of "refined flavor." There were those that were "cloudy," perhaps due to a lack of sufficient filtering of the mash after fermentation. There were "white" beers, "red" beers, and even "black" or "brown" beers. There were those that were "cut with water," "at 50 percent," "one-third," or "one-fourth," to lower the level of alcohol, which in such a warm country must not have been very high originally. Perhaps that explains, in part, the very few known cases of drunkenness.

In the tale of the *Poor Man of Nippur* (56ff),[87] when the skinflint of a mayor, instead of inviting the man at his door inside, has him chased away from his home, he first mockingly offers him, by way of refreshment, the bones and the tendons of an old goat and *some third-rate beer.*

There were also beers of different manufacture—or brands, as we would say—whose names, from this distance, no longer mean anything to us. For example, at the beginning of the eighteenth century in Mari— which, strictly speaking, was outside the Mesopotamian sphere of influence—if most people drank the common beer (*šikaru*), the king did not drink it (it is never accounted for), but drank during his daily meals in his palace, only a (local?) variety, unknown to us: *alappânu.*

Other terms escape us, as well, and we are sometimes not even sure that they truly refer to *beers.* An example is the *kurunnu*, noted only—but frequently—in the first millennium BCE, which according to all the evidence was a drink of choice but whose composition, recipe, and fabrication remain mysterious to us.

Beer was drunk frequently at meals, and it no doubt accompanied meals such as banquets that were both solemn and festive (we will return to this later), but perhaps also more modest meals, depending on the means of those drinking it. We may well surmise, however—and for good reasons—that the ancient Mesopotamians drank beer at other times without consuming any food, for social purposes and for the pleasure of drinking, either at home or elsewhere.

Like bread and daily food, beer was made in the home: each family, in other words, every woman of the house, made it, as needed, in the necessary quantities. It was drunk right out of the "vat" it was made in, which could simply be a large vessel. It was sipped from a special tube used to filter out any disagreeable impurities: there are many scenes in our iconography in which we see drinkers enjoying beer this way.

It is most likely this "domestic" character that gave birth to the veritable institution that in the first half of the second millennium was known as the "Woman Taverner's House" (*bît sabîti*), and later, as the manufacture and above all the sale of the beer was passed into the hands of the husband, the "Taverner's House" (*bît sabî*). In the event that the wife, responsible for preparing the drink every day for her family, might have made too much, and taking reserves into account, the idea was soon born of sharing it with strangers, depending on finances, and even of serving it in one's home. (Later, in the first millennium, it was offered outside the home by an innkeeper who carried it and delivered it to individuals. From this practice, the traveling vendor of drink as well as of food and other items probably emerged.) Especially during the Old Babylonian Period (first half of the second millennium), the Taverner's House, or bar, as we would call it, seems to have played a social role that we can only glimpse at: a place to gather, a bit like cafés in France, but also imparting a certain sense of freedom, as well as "communicative warmth" through the libations, even though there was an absence of truly strong liquors.

Around 1780, the king of Assyria, Šamši-Addu, vilified this institution in one of his letters (*ARM I.28:17*) as being an infamous place encouraging debauchery, sometimes even a den of iniquity. A number of representations of drinking places, showing several drinkers, straws in their mouths, around the beer "vat," reveal other, less innocent activities going on between people of opposite sexes, or sometimes the same sex. We have documentary evidence of a curious "exorcism" ritual (prayers and rituals to obtain some favor from the gods), recopied in the first millennium BCE but most likely more ancient, to be performed in order to implore the goddess Ištar, patron of physical love and its excesses, to increase the numbers of the declining clientele of the Taverner, the owner and exploiter of the place.[88] Opened first to serve beer liberally, then to enable patrons to slacken the reins a bit and let off steam, which would have been dangerous to keep under pressure, the Tavern was overseen carefully by the powers that were: revolts could be hatched there, conspiracies, plots, and Hammurabi, in his "Code" (§109ff), threatened with death any innkeeper that did not denounce such plots. Similarly he condemned any priestess who might be found there to the disgrace of the dignity of her position, which was devoted to the gods, to be burned alive.

Wine Made From Fruit

It is quite plausible that even in very ancient times the Mesopotamians learned how to press fruits containing juice, either alone or mixed together, not only dates but others that were "sugary" and flavorful, to let them ferment so as to make beverages out of them, drinks that were both more pleasing to the palate and more nutritional. A few appear to have emerged here and there in our sources. But we know almost nothing about their composition, their preparation, or their place among other beverages drunk by humans and the gods.

Wine is no doubt the most ancient and the most famous of those beverages. And, although it arrived late in Mesopotamia, we possess ample details about it.

In Sumerian it was called *geštin*, composed of *geš/giš* (which designated "wood" and everything relating to trees), and *tin*, which remains unknown to us but might have designated "life." But we see no reason at all, especially in the early eras, to confer the obviously flattering and quite enigmatic name of "tree of life" to the vine. For, in fact, *geštin* at first only designated the vine and its fruit "the grape," but not "wine," which came later. Vine, grape, and wine also had one and the same name in Akkadian: *karânu*, an old term common to all Semitic languages (this is the Hebrew *kérém*) to evoke "vine" or "vineyard."

The first time our archives unquestionably place us in the presence of *wine*, and no longer "vine" or "grape" (whose ideograms are first encountered, in very few examples, among the ancient tablets of Ur from the first third of the third millennium),[89] is in a text from the middle of the twenty-third century, in an inscription of the king of Lagaš, Uru-KA-gina (2351–2342 BCE),[90] in which he boasts, among his great deeds, of having been the very first to

> **build the beer cellar, where they brought him**
> **wine from the Mountain, in great urns.**

Here we are certainly dealing with *wine*, a liquid; and "the Mountain," in Mesopotamia, was the "High Land," the Syro-Armenian region to the north whose ancient tradition, fossilized in its way in the biblical legend of Noah (Genesis 9:20ff), had been the theater of the discovery of that noble beverage, probably due to its rich planting of vines and the abundance of grapes there. The ancient Mesopotamians long remembered that "mountainous" origin of wine. Wine was even called "beer of the Mountain" once or twice—a denomination of significance, clearly recalling the anteriority of beer.

Wine was therefore a foreigner, a latecomer, imported for centuries and eventually naturalized, but with roots elsewhere.

This is no doubt the reason why it is mentioned so infrequently in the food section on the last tablets of "the Great Encyclopedia," which since the beginning of the second millennium had in a certain sense codified the ancient local tradition; beer is the object of two hundred entries; wine, scarcely a dozen.

And it also explains that unlike the venerable Ninkasi, beer raised to the rank of the gods, wine was never deified in any way. The divinities *Geštin-anna* ("celestial vine") and *Nin-giš-zi-da* ("Lord of the True Wood," assuming that that last term refers to the vine), played only minor mythological roles, and both of their names referred not to wine but to the vine and its fruit.

A foreign product, and imported into the land mainly after the third millennium, wine, for lack of local production, gradually became integrated as an important element of trade, preferably transported by the river (it also followed the Euphrates downstream), primarily between Karkemiš, to the northeast of Alep, and Sippar, less than a hundred kilometers from Babylon. To illustrate this traffic, a few business letters survive from Babylonian merchants, represented by itinerant agents who went to select and buy the wine where it was made and followed it to the end of its voyage, seeing that it was delivered. A certain Bêlânun wrote (around 1700 BCE) to his agent Aḫûni:[91]

> Why didn't you buy and send me good wine? Buy me some, and send it to me! Then come here yourself to Babylon and see me.

And again:[92]

> A boat loaded with wine has just arrived in Sippar. Buy me 10 shekels worth [around 80 grams]. Have it delivered to me, and come see me in Babylon.

Increasingly common, but always expensive and precious since it was imported, we find mention of wine more frequently as time goes by. No doubt, people quickly learned to store it and care for it "in the cellar." Several documents, notably from Mari, appear instructive on this point, though they are not always clear.

Wine was judged, or preferred—by virtue of rather numerous criteria of taste, color, strength, and perhaps also different composition—"ripe" (literally "cooked"); "strong"; "sweet" (mixed with honey?); "clear," perhaps "white" as opposed to "red"; "with good flavor" or "of inferior quality"; the color of a "cow's eye"; and even, perhaps, to designate a product that was of very high quality, "royal beverage." "Old" wine, as opposed to "recent" wine, using the same terms that were applied to beer, was not necessarily of higher quality; it might simply have turned vinegary.

This generous vocabulary gives us a glimpse (as happens more often in the case of present-day wine experts with their specialized vocabulary) of a know-how, if not of a knowledge itself, based on great familiarity with the drink: experience with this respectable, perfectly acclimated liquid over time.

It is possible that in Mari and elsewhere, following the example of the first foreign producers, the local people themselves planted vines and picked and processed the grapes. This activity could have been possible as far as southern Mesopotamia, the heat in itself posing no obstacle.

Yet it was mainly in the north, in Assyria, that viticulture seems to have been successfully established; however, we know neither when nor how. We sometimes find mention of true *vintages*, named and described by the land where the vines were planted, and obviously valued for their specific flavors, presentation, qualities, and reputations (we can hardly discuss their "bouquet"): there was the "wine of Inzalla," "of Arnabânu," of "Hulbunu"—places that we cannot always locate but might have been in Syria or even Babylonia. The "wine of Tupliaš," for example, was a product from the valley of the Diyala. This was a famous "bitter" wine, no doubt flavored through an appropriate process, unknown to us, from some plant with a specific taste, like the almond flavor in Amaretti.

Wine became important everywhere in the land. It was drunk increasingly as time went on; and in the "menu" of the great banquet of Aššurnasirpal II, the rather prodigious quantity of wine served was the same as that for beer—one hundred thousand liters!

In spite of such progress, wine never supplanted beer, far from it (for example, it was never used in cooking). Beer had been at home in Mesopotamia since the beginning of time, not only rooted in the customs of the people but linked to their most basic agricultural product, grain. Wine, in spite of its success, seems to have been an attractive, flavorful, perhaps headier beverage, both invigorating and tempting, and increasingly appreciated; but it never dethroned the traditional beverage that had long been divinized in every sense of the word.

More than two centuries after the death of the ancient civilization of which that eminent beverage had been one of the most famous products, an obscure Middle Eastern rhetor, Julius the African, wrote in his *Kestoi* that if Dionysos, the Greek god of wine, had always refused to settle among the Babylonians and teach them to cultivate the vine and produce wine, it was because he had found them to be incorrigible drinkers of beer.

MEALS AND FEASTS

All food and drink, prepared and cooked at the cost of so much ingenuity and trouble, ended up by being presented to the eater on one of those portable platters that were called "tables" (*paššūru*) and finally consumed.

It would be pedantic to linger here on the vocabulary relating to eating and drinking, some words of which we have already touched upon. But we can never overemphasize the distinction that must be made between nourishing oneself, merely consuming food, and dining, which, among people assembled in good company, suggests much more: a sort of complicity with the food and the pleasure that it imparts, both inspired by the thought, the sight, the expectation, and the placing into one's mouth of the food and beverages, provided that the work of preparation has made them appetizing and tempting. Among the ancient Mesopotamians, as among ourselves, all the words relating to cuisine refer, of course, primarily to their concrete and mundane significance, but in certain cultures, depending on the context, they seem to have acquired a superior and in some manner sentimental value: a simple *meal*, meant to ingest food products, is transformed into a *feast*, a *banquet*, a gastronomic occasion.

Lacking any documents that describe the discreet and inaccessible daily routine of the common man, we will focus here on the crowning example of a meal, its superior state—the banquet or feast. Such a grand meal far surpasses mere physiological needs and, because it demonstrates the raison d'être of cuisine and eating, bears on psychology: from a simple mechanical activity the feast gains the rank of a cultural act.

The tale of *The Poor Man of Nippur* (mentioned above in "Drinks"), helps us to see the difference:

1   There was a man, a citizen of Nippur, destitute and poor.
     Gimil-Ninurta was his name, an unhappy man!
     In his city, Nippur, he lived, working hard, but
     Had not the silver befitting his class,
     Nor had he the gold befitting people (of his stature).
     His storage bins lacked pure grain,
     His insides burned, craving food, and
     His face was unhappy, craving meat and first-class beer;
     Having no food, he lay hungry every day, and
10   Was dressed in garments that had no change.
     In his unhappy mood, he thought to himself:
     I'll strip off my garments which have no change, and
     In my city of Nippur's market I'll buy a sheep!"
     So he stripped off his garments that had no change, and
     In his city Nippur's market he bought a three-year-old goat.
     In his unhappy mood, he thought to himself:
     Suppose I slaughter this goat in my yard—
     There could be no feast, for where is the beer?
     My friends in the neighborhood would find out and be furious,
20   And my family and relatives would be angry with me.

He obviously does not die of hunger in spite of his "poverty"; what he wants is not simple sustenance but, for once in his life, for his pleasure, to have a good meal—in other words, a *feast*.

To attain his goal he is lacking three things: meat, beer, and company. For if a meal is in itself an individual undertaking, a good meal, a feast, is a social act, implying both a shared abundance and a magnificent display.

Gimil-Ninurta thus figures that in order to obtain the feast he is dreaming about, he will provide at least part of what is lacking by offering his goat to the mayor, who is rich and privileged. For according to the custom whereby the person receiving a gift will offer one in return, the mayor will no doubt invite Gimil-Ninurta to the banquet that he will surely put on, under the circumstances. Unfortunately the goat is old and tough, and the mayor, refusing to accept such a miserable present, ignominiously dismisses Gimil-Ninurta, who then, with cunning and humor, seeks a triple vengeance—and that is what happens in the rest of the tale.

Beyond the common consumption of food, which was repetitive and uninteresting, true pleasure could be found in eating and drinking in good company, provided that the table be generously laid and festive: not only should there be bread with the foods one normally ate every day, but some unusual and succulent meat, with rivers of that euphoric beer, so that the eater would be not only satiated but full of well-being.

The *banquet* was thus first imagined as a festive occasion, a happy event, capable of erasing the concerns and the drudgery of everyday life and of filling people with contentment and joy. A feast represented something more than the simple provision of one's daily bread: it gave eating and drinking their full meaning, justifying the long work that was necessary to prepare the dishes, from the fields to the kitchen. A banquet broke with the ordinary, occasioned as it most often was by fortunate circumstances in life that were outside the daily routine and thus naturally joyful.

Tales of such festivities among simple mortals, as we have already noted, are rather rare in our cuneiform collections. But this is not the case with a few strictly historical and largely literary and mythological documents, which, in that anthropomorphist regime, merely transposed and magnified the mundane realities of daily life up to the level of the sublime divinities. In these texts, therefore, we can find an unusual documentation, a vivid and attractive image of the great circumstances of life, those that included eating and drinking.

To my knowledge, nothing has yet suggested that a *birth,* an event in itself joyous, ritually gave rise to specific celebrations or was celebrated with a meal. But one of the principal turning points in everyone's life, which has a considerable impact on communal life, everything normally occurring with good cheer, was *marriage.*

Marriage was not, of course, celebrated following the western model, least of all the modern western model. In Mesopotamian society, which was powerfully patriarchical, the decisive point in marriage was the definitive introduction of the wife into the paternal home of the husband, which would henceforth be her sole residence, theoretically until her death. It was that "introduction" that inaugurated the couple's life together. Marriage contracts (we have found a good number of them) and "codes," concerned above all with specifying a legal situation, normally teach us nothing about the "ceremony" strictly speaking that necessarily accompanied such a "passage." We only know through scattered, sometimes unclear allusions that the decisive moment was, in a sense, "sacramentalized" by two self-serving ceremonies: (1) the bride was anointed by her father, which meant he was placing her new life under the authority of the gods; and (2) in the house of the future husband, which would therefore be that of the future wife, a great festive meal was held at the expense of the husband's family. As far as I know, we haven't yet found any description of such a feast or culinary celebration.

But there is a refreshing and touching Sumerian myth from the beginning of the second millennium that fills this gap and helps us to imagine what might have occurred. *The Marriage of Sud* tells how the goddess Sud one day became the first wife—Ninlil—of the king of the gods, Enlil.[93]

Enlil falls in love with a pretty young goddess who comes from the town of Ereš and answers to the name of Sud. Believing at first that he is dealing with an easy woman, and having proposed to sleep with her, he is harshly sent packing. Once he understands his error, he immediately follows form and asks Sud's mother for her daughter's hand, according to custom. To formally present his request, he sends his agent to Sud's parents in their town:[94]

30   **Do not tarry. Repeat to her what I am going to tell you:**
      "I am an unmarried man, I send you a message concerning my wishes.
      I want to take your daughter as wife, give me your consent . . ."

Again according to the custom, he loads the agent with presents for the parents, as well as jewels for Sud.

Sud's mother agrees and orders the messenger to take her agreement to Enlil, not without having set

76   **. . . a table of rejoicing**

intended simply to ratify and celebrate agreements, as well as to honor Enlil through his envoy.

Scarcely has the latter returned, when Enlil begins feverishly to send his future in-laws, in preparation for the wedding meal, a prodigious quantity of choice foods:

104 **He raised his head toward the Upper Country, animals came running:**
      Quadrupeds, from goats to donkeys, that multiply freely in the desert.
      The uncountable ones that are in the mountain were chosen:
      Wild oxen, red deer, elephants, fallow deer, gazelles, bears, wild sheep, and rams.
      Lynxes, foxes, wild cats, tigers, mountain sheep, water buffaloes, monkeys,
      Thick-horned fat cattle that bellow,
110 **Cows and their calves, wild cattle with wide-spread horns, led by blue ropes,**
      Ewes and lambs, goats and kids, romping and fighting,
      Large kids with long beards, scratching with their hooves, lambs, [ ],
      Sheep fit for a lord, Enlil directed toward Ereš.

And to complete the feast he adds dairy products and all varieties of fruit:

114 Large cheeses, mustard-flavored cheeses, small cheeses, [ ],
     Various kinds of milk products, [ ],
     White honey, dry honey, the sweetest [ ],
     [ ] thick and large, Enlil directed toward Ereš.
     [ ], dates, figs, large pomegranates, [ ],
     Cherries, plums, halub-nuts, pistachios, acorns,
120 Dilmun dates packed in baskets, dark-colored date clusters,
     Large pomegranates seeds plucked from their rinds, big clusters of early
        grapes,
     Exotic trees in fruit, trees from orchards, [ ] grown in winter.
     Fruits from the orchards, Enlil directed toward Ereš.

These fantastic amounts primarily suggest the splendor and the abundance of the feast, which would enthrone the young princess in the supereminent position as wife of the king of the gods.

But above all, since there is nothing insignificant in these rites of passage, if the future bride and her family ate the food offered and eaten at the same time by the husband and his relatives, it was a way of affirming and creating a vital connection between them: they shared the same food to derive the same life out of it—this is the hidden and fundamental meaning of meals, and we will see this again below.[95]

This feast, therefore, only *appeared* to be a light-hearted and festive meal. In reality, in the mentality and the habits of the time (and there are many other characteristics of this mentality), it was what one might call, in quotation marks, a "sacrament": a ritual both symbolic and effective, which, taken as a whole, *symbolized* a state of affairs to be realized, in this case the visceral and fundamental link between the new bride and her husband's family, and at the same time, *created* it.

Thus beyond their obvious celebratory nature, banquets connoted *something else*, providing us with an in-depth view of the true meaning of eating and drinking. We find this meaning, in different contexts, in a few other historical ceremonies involving food, but also in the imaginary adventures recounted in myths, reflecting the behavior, the life, and the thought of human beings.

Let us begin with the most famous feast, the most fabulous, the most Pantagruelian. This banquet was offered by the Assyrian king Aššurnasirpal II (883–859 BCE) to celebrate the completed renovation of the town of Kalḫu/Nimrud, which he had chosen as his new capital. The king had assumed responsibility for providing food and drink for ten days for *sixty-nine thousand five hundred seventy-four guests:* his high-ranking bureaucrats and the population of Kalḫu, with a respectable number of allies and neighbors, plus all those who had worked to restore the city and its monuments. Here, on the stele that bears the text,[96] is the list of foodstuffs required for this astounding meal: not only does it give an idea of what a banquet of that time might have been, but it illustrates very well, if we pay close attention, the hierarchy and even the ordering of the foodstuffs, as is highlighted by a brief commentary:

102 At the time when Aššurnasirpal, king of Assyria, adorned the palace, the joy of the heart, even a palace embodying all the skill of Kalḫu, and when he invited into it Aššur, the great lord, and the gods

105 of all the land [to a banquet, the menu of which is as follows, beginning with the meat]: 1,000 barley-fed oxen, 1,000 young cattle, and sheep from the stalls, 14,000 common sheep (from the flocks) belonging to Ištar my mistress, 200 oxen, from (the herds) belonging to Ištar my mistress, 1,000 fattened sheep,

110 1,000 lambs, 500 deer; 500 gazelles, 1,000 large birds, 500 geese; 500 fowls, 1,000 *suki*-birds, 1,000 *qaribe*-birds, 10,000 pigeons, 10,000 doves, 10,000 small birds, 10,000 fishes, 10,000 locusts(?),

115 10,000 eggs . . .

Then comes the bread-based food, comparatively not as abundant, but we are not told either the size nor the weight involved:

10,000 loaves.

Then we have the drinks: again, in a relatively small quantity, with the possible addition of water always implied:

10,000 (measures of) beer; 10,000 (skins) of wine.

What comes next is quite varied and appears to have been what we would call "accompaniments," "condiments," "garnish," and the like, among which it is not easy—indeed it is neither possible nor necessary—to introduce subcategories, about which we know almost nothing:

116 . . .10,000 cuttings of *šu'*—corn (and) sesame, 10,000 *lummu*-vessels of. . . . 1,000 garden-produced *habarahu*, 300 (measures of) carob-pods, 300 ŠEMUN, 300 (of) spiced herbs,

120 100 alkali-salt, (100) . . . salt, 100 roasted-barley, 100 *uhšennu*-grain, 100 (measures of) fine mixed beer, 100 pomegranates, (grapes from) 100 *išhunatu*-vines, 100 mixed jujubes, 100 pistachio-nuts, 100 *kussi*

125   100 garlic, 100 wild-onions, 100 lentils, 100 . . . of turnip, 200 ḫinḫinu-
grain, 100 . . . of 100 AM, 100 himetu-ghee, 100 fresh roasted barley, 100
roasted šu'-corn, 100 karkartu

130   100 tiatu, 100 roses, 100 milk, 100 eqidi, 100 šappu-pots of mizi, 100
arsuppu-cereal soused, 10 homers [1 homer = approx. 100 gallons.—
Trans.] kulli of dukdu, 20 homers kulli of pistachio-nuts, 10 homers of
kussi-fruit, 10 homers of castor-oil pods(?),

135   10 homers of dates, 10 homers of figs, 10 homers of cumin, 10 homers of
cress, 10 homers of aniseed, 10 homers andahšu-lentils, of mock
pepper(?), 10 homers of šumittalu, 10 homers of hakamu, 10 homers of
fine oil, 20 homers of fine spices, 10 homers of aubergine, 10 homers of
anemones,

140   10 homers of zinzime-vetches, 10 homers of bitter almonds. When I
adorned the palace of Kalḫu 47,074 workmen and women summoned
from all the districts of my land; 5,000 high officials, the envoys of the
Suhi, Hindanaeans, Hattinaeans, Hittites, Tyrians,

145   Sidonians, Gurgumeans, Malideans, Hubuskaeans, Gilzaneans,
Kumeans, Musasiraeans. 16,000 persons (souls) of Kalḫu, 1,500 zariqu-
officials of all my palaces. The total was 69,574.

150   The Happy peoples of all the lands together with the people of Kalḫu for
ten days I feasted, wined, bathed, anointed and honored them and then
sent them back to their lands in peace and joy.

We must not, of course, imagine this feast as we would think of a modern
dinner party, with guests sitting quietly side by side at a table that has
been set to do honor to the host's generosity, for the king's feast lasted
ten days, and, moreover, the king took it upon himself to provide all this
food and drink. This is not an *account* of the festivities, but a *list* of the
foods provided magnificently by the king.

Moreover, when we look at the quantities closely, they indicate that
there must have been more than one *menu*: how would you divide ten
thousand eggs among seventy thousand guests?

But what matters for us is not the ordering of the banquet, but the responsibility assumed by the king on this festive occasion to provide food
and drink for his people.

It must be pointed out that this occasion is not the only such example
in history, although it is, in my opinion, the most detailed. Already,
around the end of the twenty-fifth century, King Lagaš, Ur-Nanše (2494–
2465 BCE), had congratulated himself in one of his inscriptions (*IRSA*, p.
46: IC3ff) for the inauguration of the temple of Ningirsu, for having

had 70 *kur* of barley eaten in the temple,

in other words, more than 300 hectoliters, mentioning only the bread—which implies an amazing feast.

It is quite possible that such great feasts offered by kings to their subjects, for various occasions, were in some respects taken for granted and thus institutionalized. The sumptuous meals that the illustrious Sargon of Akkad (around 2350 BCE) offered daily to his 5,400 men are recalled in that king's own inscriptions,[97] and became a subject of legend that the Assyrian merchants who had expatriated to Anatolia still told each other at their gatherings some 500 years later:

> By Addad and Ištar, I swear it! [it is Sargon speaking]
> Every day I sacrificed a thousand cattle and it was
> seven thousand of my gallant knights who, every day, ate
> chops with me.[98]

We can also recall here the accounts for the "daily meals" of the king of Mari, which more than once were shared with his subjects;

> Meals of the king and his people.

We should not interpret "his people" in the military sense as "his troops" (who are sometimes mentioned explicitly, moreover), but quite simply as a choice of representatives of his people. Marking the solemnity of the occasion, these documents sometimes mention not only gifts that were simultaneously presented to the guests, but also the distribution of oils and perfume so that the guests could wash up properly in accordance with the official solemnity of the event.

Such great meals that the king shared with (representatives of) his subjects, necessarily implied something other than the simple sharing of food and drink, as we can see if we simply look beyond the words to consider their meaning. These generous meals were immediately connected to the very function and role of the sovereign:

> 40 The great gods have called me,
> and I am indeed the good shepherd who brings peace with the just
>   scepter.
> 46 My benevolent shade covered my city!
> I have carried in my bosom
> 50 The people of Sumer and Akkad:
> Thanks to my good fortune, they have prospered!
> 55 I have not ceased to administer them in peace:
> By my wisdom I have harbored them.[99]

All this more spectacular largesse associated with a meal recalled both the beneficent power of the king, who provided it, and the vital importance of remaining happily subject to his advantageous authority. On another level, feasts and festivities were *eminently political acts.*

Such gatherings could therefore serve as frameworks for assemblies and political decision-making. We lack historical data, I believe, but we are largely compensated by the information found in myths.

One of the most convincing examples of this is provided in the *Epic of Creation.*[100] In this tale, when the young and active generation of gods see themselves in danger of being exterminated by the great primal Mother, Tiamat, along with her fearsome hoard and the support of the ancient, sedentary, gods, they begin looking for a defender and champion, and set their sights on the powerful young Marduk. Their "dean," Anšar, then summons them together for a salutory debate, which takes place during a meal.

> 7 "Let them bring all the gods before me.
> "Let them converse, sit down at a feast,
> "On produce of the field let them feed, imbibe [beer],
> 10 "Let them ordain destiny for Marduk, their champion.[101]

In other words, they were to decide together and during a large meal to invest Marduk to defend them—and save them.

The banquet was thus also a sort of Arthurian "Round Table," where the sharing of food and drink engendered good fellowship and good understanding, energizing a discussion so that an otherwise difficult decision (that was wise and salutory) could be made:

> 130 All the great gods . . . came before Anšar,
>   and were filled with [joy].
> One kissed the other in the assembly [   ],
> They conversed, sat down at a feast,
> On produce of the field they fed, imbibed [beer]
> 135 With sweet liquor they made their gullets run,
> They felt good from drinking beer.
> Most carefree, their spirits rose,
> 138 To Marduk their champion they ordained destiny.[102]

The rest details how they thus put Marduk at their head and treated him as a chief, at least a military chief.

This could not be better said or better described, that is, how good-humored conviviality due to the united presence of all those who share the same life, along with a good euphoric meal and delicate "intoxicating beverages," inspires solidarity and understanding, sources of unanimous decisions, those that are the most serious and most difficult to make, but also the most critical.

This is confirmed in a final scene: after Marduk has conquered and slain Tiamat, and even, thanks to his intelligence, benevolence, and energy (which were expected of him), has gone beyond what was expected and constructed the universe out of the remains of that monstrous goddess, has installed the gods there, each in his place, and, as his final and supreme good work, has invented man to perform the gods' labor for them (this is a rewriting of the version from *Altrahasis*),[103] the gods, enthusiastic and full of gratitude, are prepared not only to keep him as their leader, but to promote him to king of the entire universe, of both gods and humans. Then Marduk, by virtue of his supreme position and as if to enthrone himself on this occasion, invites all the gods to a great banquet, which this time he organizes and presides over himself:

69 The Lord, on the Exalted Dais,
    which they built as his dwelling [that is, Babylonia and its major temple
      of Esagil],
    Seated the gods his fathers for a banquet.
    The great gods sat down,
75 They set out cups, they sat down at the feast.[104]

It was thus during this grandiose and euphoric feast that the gods proceeded to definitively invest Marduk, who was no longer merely their captain, but was now their sovereign. They transferred all power to him, in the form of "names" that they imposed on him, each of which truly *contained*, following the beliefs of the time, the prerogatives it *conveyed*.

On close examination, eating and drinking, cuisine and meals, thus gradually appear to be much more important; they are no longer just routines that maintain physical life. Not only do we realize that the huge amount of physical labor they required rapidly opened up onto an entire realm of professional techniques, a complicated and knowledgeable expertise that even led to artistic creations—a specific, though perhaps rudimentary, cult of "the beautiful." But the sharing of meals could also intervene, quite powerfully, in social and political life.

We will now see that eating and drinking also held an important place in the religious life of ancient Mesopotamia.

THE TABLE OF THE GODS

In an anthropomorphist culture such as that of the ancient Mesopotamians, the gods, imagined by way of a human model, necessarily ate and drank just as humans did, but better. Thus human mores and customs were applied to the gods on the scale of their superexcellence, in all appropriate realms of existence, including eating and drinking, which were believed necessary for the gods' lives to be sustained.

We have had the opportunity, if we believe the myths, to learn how the gods' feasts were arranged. In place of documentary sources, however, let us consult first the *liturgical rituals*, which were transposed from court etiquette and of which we have already seen a little: these recorded both the programs and the codes of the gods' "maintenance," their *cult*.

According to traditional belief, from the beginning of time this "maintenance" was the sole responsibility and the essential duty of humans. In order to imagine better the realism, fervor, and pomp behind the ritual, it is useful first to recall a very beautiful, intelligent, and revealing myth, recorded in Akkadian, which explains and justifies the ritual and involves a legendary ancient ruler who gave the tale its name: *Atraḫasîs*, literally "Supersage."

This long poem,[105] in its first complete versions, must have been "1,250 lines" long, as pointed out in the conclusion of one of those versions. To date we have recovered around three-fourths of it, enough to follow and sufficiently study the entire work. We had been unable to grasp the general sense of the scattered fragments that had been gradually recovered over more than one hundred years when, in 1965, the British Assyriologist W. G. Lambert discovered and published the remains of the oldest known manuscript of this work, which had been lying dormant since 1889 in the drawers of the British Museum. This manuscript, as we are told in the final note, had been

recopied by Kasap(?)-Aya, junior scribe,
on the 21st of the first month of the fifth year
of the reign of Ammi-sadûqa, king of Babylon,

in other words (this ruler is dated around 1640 BCE), only a few dozen years after the poem was composed in Babylon, or not far from there, we believe.

Highly valued in its own land, as is indicated by its numerous copies or rewritings until not far from the common era, Atraḫasîs, in the approximately forty fragments of it that we have recovered over the years, is a masterpiece of the religious thought—and of the thought in general—of the ancient Mesopotamians. We can measure its importance and its "authority" even beyond its native cultural milieu by the fact that it made its way into the Bible, where it formed the framework for the first chapters of Genesis, which also tell of the origins and the first history of mankind. Its presence in the Bible, however, has not been admitted without an energetic attempt to harmonize it with the great principles, fiercely monotheistic and "moral," of the religion of Israel.

The tale of Atraḫasîs begins without preliminaries in the time when the human race did not yet exist; only the gods were present. And, like every society that sees itself clearly, the Mesopotamians saw their gods' society as being composed of two great "classes:" at the top were the chiefs, the greatest gods, who never worked but only governed the world; and beneath them, the others, the divine lower class, forced by their superiors for the common good to dedicate themselves to manual labor for all the necessary things in life by exploiting the natural riches of the earth.

That was an excessive, exhausting, and ultimately humiliating occupation. So one fine day the worker gods decide they have had enough and go on strike, no longer accepting the inequality that has been keeping them apart from the privileged idleness of their leaders. There is great panic in the divine world: if no one does anything any more, there will be scarcity, hunger, famine.

The wisest of the great gods, Enki/Ea, then devises and proposes a plan to save them: they will have to create a substitute for the striking gods—a creature that alone will accomplish the work in their place but can never claim, as the "strikers" did, promotion to the ruling gods' condition. The creature will therefore be made out of clay and thus destined to die. In that land, and we can well understand why, dying was called "returning to clay," becoming clay again. In order that this substitute, which would be a human, could best fulfill his mission, the clay was kneaded with "the flesh and blood" of a lower-ranking god so that the raw material of the human would be elevated by intelligence and energy to the level of the work to be done.

Applauded by the gods, the project was immediately undertaken. Since the rest of the story of *Atraḫasîs* does not relate to our subject, we will leave it aside. But what comes out of the part just described is that humans were invented, composed, and created by the gods to be their servants, eminent and unique, with the principal duty of producing through their multiform work all the goods necessary to assure the gods a worry-free and beatific life, thereby leaving the gods free, without any other concern, to attend to their primary function: the governance of the world. It was up to humans, then, to provide the gods with opulent and splendid residences—temples—and with the rarest and most costly sacred furnishings; the most sought-after undergarments, clothing, and ornamentation; and above all, since this was their primary and fundamental need, food and drink, the most abundant and delectable that could be provided.

This is what is called the *maintenance of the gods*, which constituted in large part the religion of those people, their *cult*.

Here, too, we must rid ourselves of the traditional thinking about religious behavior that the Bible has more or less instilled in us. In the presence of a unique and transcendent God who needs nothing and desires nothing, the Bible has taught us that what we might feel compelled to offer to him, to sacrifice to him out of a generous impulse inspired by our religious feeling, must be thought of as being governed by a sense of sacrifice and renunciation, which leads to the total annihilation of the "gift," the "burnt offering." Biblical sacrifice, the idea of which we have become more or less accustomed to, is basically a *negative* gesture: it deprives us—and we willingly accept this deprivation—of something we reserve for God without his having a need or a use for it. In Mesopotamia, on the other hand, sacrifice, offerings to the gods, were *positive* actions: what was given to them, they needed. They demanded it, appropriated it, and, as regards food, were believed to eat it (even if, in fact, people other than the gods necessarily did so in their place). Sacrifice was truly a gift, an offering. The Akkadian vocabulary for "sacrifice" revolved around two notions that, each in its own way, emphasized such a transfer: *naqû*, "to pour" a liquid that was being offered as a drink; and *mahâru*, "to receive," to accept what was thus offered.

Receive, Šamaš, the beer that is poured for you,

as is expressed in a famous hymn to that god.[106]

To ensure the "maintenance" of the gods, the most essential goods, the most continually indispensable, were those that would above all maintain their *lives*, those things for which all humans, all *living creatures*, have a constant and imperative need: food and drink.

This is what I call the "table of the gods," the primary preoccupation and basic concern of the Mesopotamian cult whose ceremonial bears directly on the subject of the present book.

It is an established fact, and one without a remedy, that the ritual of the cult in that land, in spite of countless allusions to it in wide-ranging contexts, is almost unknown as a whole and in its logic, especially as one goes back farther in time. We glean a few scraps of it here and there, such as this dedication on a silver vessel in a temple by the king of Lagaš, Entemena (2404–2375 BCE), in one of his commemorative inscriptions:[107]

> For Ningirsu, the champion of Enlil,
> Entemena, the Prince of Lagaš,
> The elect of the heart of Nanše,
> The son of Enanatum . . . ,
> Had this pitcher of pure silver made,
> So that Ningirsu could enjoy his butter in it.

This suggests a ritual practice during which the god was believed to taste some refined food.

And in this excerpt from a Sumerian myth from the end of the third millennium, it is striking that the departure of Enki, who leaves in order to look over his territory and keep it in good order, was accompanied by liturgical lustrations from his sanctuary:[108]

> 140 For the great prince [Enki] who comes forth in (his) land,
> All the lords, all the chieftains,
> The incantation-priests
> Those who wear linen-garments in Sumer,
> They perform of the purification rites of the *apsû*
> 145 To father Enki, they set their feet in the pure place, in the land,
> They [purify] the dwelling for him . . .
> They call his (name) in the "stations,"
> They purify the lofty shrine of the *apsû*
> In its midst they cause to come forth the tall juniper-tree, the pure plant.

In our state of documentary poverty, with a few rare images gleaned here and there, we must make do with what we have. Lacking archaic accounts, we invoke more recent documents while appealing to the well-known rule of the universal immobility of religious practice, whose codified gestures, perhaps first inspired by court protocol, have most probably been perpetuated without much change throughout the centuries, as is suggested, once or twice, by the appearance of out-of-place characteristics from another age.

To best illustrate "the table of the gods" and its common practice, we present a famous tablet from the Seleucid period, two or three centuries BCE, a time when the lofty civilization of the land was gradually being extinguished, although the daily lives of its inhabitants, its rulers, and its gods seem to have undergone no sudden change. This document was discovered with a number of others at Uruk, the venerable city where it had been copied and used. It recorded the ceremonial practices of the era, the final stage of a long tradition that had no doubt remained more or less unchanged; we may therefore feel justified in examining it.

Published by Fr. Thureau-Dangin, starting on page 74 of his *Rituels accadiens*, the tablet applied directly only to the great temples of Uruk and to the few major divinities that resided and were honored there—a dozen or so, at most. It conveys marvelously the duty that the "servants" of the gods performed there to *maintain* them, in other words, primarily to feed them, naturally every day since that is a necessity of nature. Following a procedure that was both ceremonial and economic (the administrators of the sanctuaries must have planned for their needs), the text accounts for, and tallies up, the items necessary for a year of those daily meals by recalling and specifying that there were four of them, at least for people with means: a small and a large meal before midday and a small and a large one after midday—we have no way of knowing their schedule, or even which one of the two came first. We have already looked at the first paragraph dealing with beverages, noting that the guests were quite generously served—some twenty liters of top-quality drinks per meal and per person. The rest, as we shall soon see, was comparable.

After the *drinks*, and to conform to a certain logic in dining, there were *grain products* (obverse 21–47, pp. 76 and 81), *fruits* (48–50, pp. 77 and 83), then *meats* (reverse 1ff). That was of course only the foundation of the meal, so to speak. What was always essential, and present, were the dishes that constituted the meal "gastronomically" and came under another authority, another program, and thus another ritual, about which we know nothing—and this is unfortunate for our culinary curiosity.[109]

F.21 **Every day of the whole year, for the principal regular offerings there will be needed 648 liters of barley and spelt.**

These "regular offerings," imposed by the liturgical tradition that established each guest's share, are recorded on the tablet; the nutritional "service" and "maintenance" of every god of Uruk are tallied up as accurately as possible:

23   Such is the total that the millers will provide daily to the temple cooks, in the kitchen [let us not forget that the bakery was part of the kitchen] for the four (daily) meals of the gods.

Then there are the details of what the "cooks" were to make out of this mass of flour in order to prepare bread for the gods, the very foundation of their diet, as it was for humans.

25   From the above they will take 486 liters of barley flour and 162 liters of spelt flour, from the mixture of which the cooks will prepare and bake [epû] 243 "round loaves." Out of that total the same cooks will prepare and deliver 30 round loaves for the table of Anu: that is, each time 8 loaves for the large and the small morning meals, and 7 for the large and small afternoon meals.

30   30 loaves will also be needed for the meals of Antu; 30 for those of Ištar; 30 for Nanaya; and 15 for the four meals of the divinities in their company. 12 for "the throne of Anu," and for the domestic divinities of the Cella of Anu; 16 for the two tiaras of Anu; 16 for the leveled tower [= the ziqqurat] and its domestic divinities; 16 for those of the two Wings of the Sanctuary of Anu and Antu. Which makes, in all, 160 loaves.

In addition to the four principal divine characters—Anu and the goddesses Antu, Ištar, and Nanaya, who were to be fed first—it was necessary to plan on a certain number of associated meals, whose beneficiaries are not very clear, though they were obviously "divine": their "service," their "maintenance," had to be accompanied by an entire ceremonial, also unclear and, in any case, beyond the scope of the present study.

Of interest to us, on the other hand, is that each of the great gods to be fed were given thirty loaves every day, the weight of which, for lack of specifics, we can guess to be at least a few kilograms. We do not know the extent to which the same guest partook of other meals. In any case, as regards the bread served to accompany his or her meals, each god was overabundantly served.

The "sacred" nature of such food and of the work to be devoted to it is emphasized in the final part of the last paragraph:

44   When [the miller] mills the above-mentioned grain, he must in doing so recite the formula: "O celestial Plow! In the field, we harnessed the seeder plow!" And, while kneading the dough, and putting it in the oven

to make loaves the cook will recite this formula: "O Nisaba! [goddess and patron of grain] Holy Abundance! Rich Allowance!"

Then, in a few words, the second part of the menu plan is devoted to the "fruits" to be served during the meals, but we don't know in what order they were served. It is striking that vegetables are never mentioned; nor, concerning the grain seen above, does there appear to have been any of those "porridges" that were so enjoyed in that land, if we are to believe our recipes. Apart from the baking of bread, nothing that relates specifically to cooking is found in the menu set out here:

48   All year long [which means that at least some of these fruits were not fresh, but dried, according to usages seen elsewhere]; every day, there will be offered to Anu, Antu, Ištar, and Nanaya, as well as to the other gods who live in Uruk, 450 liters of top quality dates: dates from Tilmum [reputed to be the best!], figs and grapes, in addition to "candy" (?) and sweets (?).

Those last two terms, poorly documented, must refer to confections or "sweet" dishes of some sort, probably made from fruit.

   The text fails to specify whether the 450 liters were to be shared among all the guests, which does not seem to conform to the style or abundance in the rest of the tablet, where each number denotes a single individual's share: that must be the case here, and it is not surprising if we consider the quantities of the other products attributed to each god.

   At the end of the tablet and its worthy crowning, there is mention of the usual meats from small and large animals, which, along with bread, made up the main substance of meals. We already have a rather clear idea of this through the "menus" of banquets, and through our recipes. It should be noted that how these meats were cooked—whether roasted or "cooked in fatty broth"—is not specified anywhere, for that point must have been determined earlier, either by procedures or by lost liturgical directions or by the inventive imaginations of the cooks.

R.1   Here is the detail of the cattle and the sheep of the regular offerings, which, every day of the whole year, must be offered to Anu, Antu, Ištar, Nanaya, and the other divinities that reside in the main temples of Uruk. For the large morning meal, for the whole year: 7 choice sheep, fattened and without flaw,

5   fed for two years on barley and 1 sheep that has been specially raised, fattened and milk-fed; or, in all, 8 sheep for regular offerings. Then, 1 large cow; 1 milk-fed calf, and 10 fattened sheep, worth less than the earlier ones, and not fed on barley. Or, in all, for the large morning meal

the entire year (every day), 18 sheep, of which 1 has been specially raised; 1 large cow and 1 milk calf.

Then there is a new reference to the liturgical nature of the culinary procedures for which it was necessary to call upon approval from on high:

> While slaughtering these cattle and sheep, the butcher will recite the formula:
>
> 10 "The son of Šamaš the master of livestock, Has caused the pasture land on the steppe to grow!"
>
> 11 *Item*, while slaughtering cattle and sheep, the head butcher will greet Anu, Antu, the Great Star [Jupiter?] and Delebat [Venus]. But he will say nothing to the other divinities. At the small morning meal . . . for the whole year, each day, will be offered 6 fattened sheep without flaw, fed on barley for two years;
>
> 15 1 large sheep, fed on milk; and 5 large sheep, but of lesser value and not fed on barley; 1 large steer; 8 lambs; 5 ducks, fed on mash; 2 ducks of lesser value; 8 geese fed on mash; 4 dormice; 30 *marratu*-birds (?); 30 turtledoves (?) . . . ; 4 reed boars; 3 ostrich eggs and 3 duck eggs.

Meat was thus if not more abundant, at least more varied, for the "small morning meal" than for the "large."

> At the large evening meal . . . every day of the whole year, will be offered 4 fattened sheep, without flaw, fed on barley for two years;
>
> 15 1 specially raised sheep . . . , fattened and raised on milk; 5 second-grade sheep and of lesser value, not fed on barley; and 10 turtledoves (?). At the small evening meal, for the same gods, for the whole year (each day): 4 fattened sheep, without flaw, fed on barley
>
> 20 for two years; 1 specially raised sheep, fed on milk; and 5 second-grade sheep of lesser value, not fed on barley.

Then, following custom, the authors draw up the subtotal of all the meats served to the gods, "every day of the whole year, at the four meals," and the quantity is impressive even though it concerns several divine guests, but not more than around ten:

> 21 top-grade sheep, fattened and without flaw, fed on barley
>
> 25 for two years; 4 specially raised sheep, fed on milk; 25 second-grade sheep not fed on milk; 2 large steers; 1 milk-fed calf; 8 lambs; 30 *marratu* (?) birds; 20 turtledoves (?); 3 mash-fed geese; 5 ducks fed on flour mash; 2 second-grade ducks; 4 dormice; 3 ostrich eggs and 3 duck eggs.

In itself this already constitutes a rather prodigious menu: the bread alone, 651 liters per meal and per person, and some 60 pieces of livestock, to which were added fruit, drinks, and probably a number of additional cooked dishes, even other parallel meals offered on the occasion of the many ceremonies and celebrations in the "liturgical year," about which we know little.

This document at least gives an authentic idea of the ostentatious and extraordinary generosity that prevailed in Mesopotamia with respect to the "maintenance of the gods," the principal duty of humans, in the realm of dining and cuisine.

The overall effect can be further magnified if we simply think of *all the gods* in *all* the sanctuaries everywhere who were similarly or equitably served: oceans of both culinary and material wealth must have overflowed in the temples "every day of the whole year." And the first duty of sovereigns—as inscriptions to their honor often boast—was to keep an eye on the constant luxury and magnificence of such outlay.

These people did not, however, go beyond their means, and we have no evidence that they ever felt pressured in their duty—which doesn't mean that they never were!

We possess copious archives dating from the end of the third millennium that preserve a portion of the accounting documents from the livestock yards concentrated in Puzriš-Dagan, a few kilometers to the south of Nippur and very close to its temples, in particular the most sublime among these and one of the most famous in the whole land, mainly in the earliest era: *Ekur*, "Mountain Temple," dedicated to the "king of gods," Enlil. Those yards provided the livestock necessary for the nutritional maintenance of the gods (among other clients) "every day of the whole year" for liturgies and other highly festive occasions. A system of tithes and taxation applied throughout the land ensured a continuous supply—in modest units or in dozens, hundreds, or even thousands—of the animals intended for the table of the gods. Here is one selection:

For the ceremony of the first of the month, there were sent:
——from the town of Umma: 6 three-year-old steers; 24 two-year old cows; 360 liters of clarified butter, and as much cheese;
——from the town of Maškan-Dudu: 240 sheep; 240 ewes; 180 lambs; 120 female lambs; 60 pigs;
——from the town of Bàd-an: 180 sheep; 420 ewes; 120 lambs; 120 female lambs; 60 pigs;
——from the town of Maškan-šapir: 120 sheep; 120 lambs; 120 female lambs; 120 kids;

——from the town of Uru-sagrig: 40 sheep and 20 ewes;
——from the town of Isin: 30 sheep and 20 ewes.
   Inventory of the governor of the town of Sippar.[110]

An annoying, but irreparable fact is the silence of the sources, which hides the rest of the economic data from us, beginning with those relating to agricultural products. One cannot imagine the quantities of such edible products, which would be even more dizzying, no doubt, if we knew all the details!

For the very notion of the "maintenance of the gods" as we understand it, and the magnanimity of its exercise, could only have been born and have prospered in a land that was economically prosperous—and the ancient Mesopotamians obviously knew what eating really meant.

The information we possess, as already mentioned, refers to the raw materials, so to speak, of eating and drinking. But those products were not served as such at the gods' table; they had first to pass through the hands of numerous "temple cooks" in their vast culinary laboratories.

We can say almost nothing about their activity under those circumstances, nor what they derived from the products that were "brought to their kitchens," so overabundantly. No doubt they often resorted to "direct cooking"—grilling and roasting—as the gods seemed to have preferred those archaic methods. But not far from the "grilled meat" (*šuwû*) in our rituals and menus there also appeared "boiled meat" (*šilqu*), indirectly cooked in broth, naturally "fatty," fresher, richer, more refined and flavorful.

Lacking more and better documentation, we must at least point out (which may add a certain meaning to our "collections" of recipes) that on more than one occasion we find traces of a liturgical reference in them—which naturally does not mean that they related only to that domain:

To prepare a bird slaughtered for a *temru* ceremony (Bii21),

temru being a term used in Mari around 1750 BCE, whose precise meaning we don't know. Or

To prepare a francolin for a . . . [ ] (Biv:1)

in which the word broken off must belong to liturgical vocabulary. Similarly in C:42, the partly restored term *mâ[kalu]*, may also refer to a "cult meal."

But these references to the cult found in our three Yale Tablets are too scattered and uncertain to lead to the conclusion that all our recipes are theocentric, as if they were all primarily intended only for the table of the gods. The little we have been able to derive in this regard suggests the *possibility* of a "sacred" use, of recipes *usable* in the temple.

In other words, the cuisine regarding which we have uncovered a sizable number of detailed documents, sumptuous in its presentation, could have been prepared and perhaps was prepared mainly for the gods; but it was also, perhaps primarily, prepared not in the temple kitchens but in those of the palaces or "manors" of ancient Mesopotamia, conveying the refined taste for the pleasures of the palate among the well-off of this world and hence, through a natural transposition, among the gods as well.

There remains a question that has barely been raised but must inevitably be asked in the presence of a "table of the gods" filled with so much food, which must have involved the efforts of culinary activity and talent: What became of those mountains and rivers of food and drink? As noted in the Uruk tablet just cited, once all that food had been assembled and transformed in the kitchen, it was "placed," with its accompaniments, "on the table" of, or "in front of," the divinity for whom it was intended. And then what?

The full mechanics of what followed elude us: they are not, to my knowledge, described in detail anywhere. But it can be well assumed that after the food had been presented to its intended gods, those who actually served the feasts, the members of the clergy serving the temple, may have taken it back to enjoy it themselves or in the company of their immediate entourage. Probably following an established routine, they either kept it or preferably sold it to others—depending on the temple finances.

In the end, the gods were believed to be filled and satisfied, were considered appropriately "maintained," simply because their "servants" had undertaken all that work and had exhibited generosity and expense in providing their "maintenance." There could not have been any other outcome, moreover, in a system that straddled the real and the imaginary, that conferred an independent and objective existence and life to nonexistent, totally imagined entities. Furthermore, to our knowledge no one ever appears to have had a serious problem with this notion.

THE TABLE OF THE DEAD

According to the ancient Mesopotamians, the dead did not fall into nothingness—an abstract, abstruse, and somewhat inaccessible notion. Once their bodies had been buried and were beginning to "return to clay" (their raw material, due to the calculations and will of Enki/Ea, when he had created humans), only a slight trace of each body remained, like an intangible, wispy shadow, imagined from the memories and dreams in which their descendants still saw them. They were called *eṭemmu*, from the Sumerian *gedim*, "ghost," "shadow," "specter," and the Mesopotamians, like many others, fantasized about it over the millennia, gradually constructing this representation, its existence and its framework, on the image of the living, but considerably blurred by the sleep, drowsiness, and immobility of the cadaver. The *eṭemmu*, like a living person on earth, had its own usual place of residence, in the company of its countless fellows, in the inferior space of the immense cosmic spheroid, the netherworld, the immeasurable, sinister cave, black, earthy, and silent: *Arallû*, as it was called.

The "ghost" was believed still to experience hunger and thirst, even if the quantities of food it would henceforth need were negligible and basically symbolic. It is upon this notion that a "cult" was established, a "maintenance of the dead," with each family, primarily the head of the family, responsible for its own deceased members. Upon the burial of a family member, a few scraps of food and a little water were placed next to the body to sustain it, sustenance that was renewed from time to time, according to a ritual about which we know almost nothing. Sometimes a sort of clay tube (*arûtu*) was placed in the tomb so that a little water could be poured from above into the dead person's mouth. Any interruption in or neglect of these almost insignificant offerings ignited the anger and bitterness of the "ghost," which, abandoned by his family, would certainly avenge itself.

For the dead remained forever connected to their families: death in no way broke the ties of blood and family life.

In the tale of the poor man of Nippur we saw that a gathering of family members around the table for a pleasant meal accompanied by an enjoyable beer was a dreamed-of scenario that would engender harmony, communication, and good common understanding. It is therefore not surprising that this scenario became the theater of a particular ceremony, noted rather frequently in our sources, called *kispu*.

This Akkadian term, related to the verb *kasâpu*: "to break in pieces and distribute," referred to the sharing of food during a common meal, to which each person brought his portion. The *kispu* therefore represented a celebration, more precisely a *meal*, and it was essential, under the circumstances, that it be shared by all the members of the same family, living and dead, who thus celebrated together. Possibly its Sumerian equivalent, *ki-sì-ga:* "placed on the ground," first designated offerings, mainly consumable, that were "placed on the ground," thus within the reach of the inhabitants of the netherworld.

Whatever the case may have been, it was a true meal of the dead, in which all the members of a family were ritually to take part, physically for the living and "mystically" for the dead, even if the passing of time allowed only a vague and distant collective memory of the dead. The ceremony must have unfolded—but we know nothing about it—as imaginatively as did that of the gods' consumption of the food presented to them.

The *kispu* was usually celebrated on the last day of every month (the Mesopotamians had a lunar calendar with thirty days in each month), at the moment when the moon, suddenly absent, turned minds and hearts to thoughts of death and the dead. But the *kispu* could also be celebrated on other convivial and familial occasions, though we hardly know why and when. It always remained primarily a *meal*, possibly with other common activities added, such as the exchange of gifts. This type of meal was basically a funeral ritual, not that of placing a body into the earth, but the rediscovery or remembrance of those who were gone, and simultaneously a reaffirmation of the solidarity of the family.

At least on the official level, the awareness of such cohesion could go beyond the realm of the family and overflow into a sense of belonging to the same community, the same people, subjects of the same king: it became a means for political solidarity.

We possess a tablet from the first half of the second millennium, which is enlightening in this regard.[111] It concerns a meal of the dead, in other words, a *kispu*, organized by the king of Babylon, Ammiṣaduqa (1646–1626 BCE), with the intent of providing food to share among the dead members of his dynasty and of earlier dynasties that were believed to have prolonged his own either directly or indirectly, but also to provide food for the dead of his people, especially those who had served their king and had perished in his service, whose descendants might have deprived them of sufficiently generous offerings from their "cult."

29   The *palū* [ghostly members] of the Amorites, the *palū* of the Haneans, the
      palū of the Gutium, the palū not recorded on this tablet, and the
      soldier(s) who fell while on *perilous campaigns* for their lord; princes,
35   princesses, all "persons" from East to West, who have [no one to take
      care of you and ensure your cult]: Come ye, eat this, drink this (meal)
      and bless Ammiṣaduqa (who is offering it to you).

I have always been moved by this touching and unexpected text, written by those venerable ancestors, so separate from us, and who still seem to be as impassive as their old stone images: we hear them call to their old forgotten dead, from the most illustrious to the most wretched. All—and this, too, is touching—are summoned in the same way by the king to a meal that he has had prepared for them to ease their pitiful hunger and thirst, even though what they needed was henceforth only negligible—unlike what was needed to satisfy the solid appetites of living people and their insatiable gods. Eating and drinking was also important for the dead.

There is even a well-known myth that teaches us two things: first, that the gods also celebrated the same "family meal," the *kispu*, around the table every month. Then, through the account of this institution, we learn what the faithful saw as the real meaning, the "ontological" meaning if you will, of eating and drinking for both humans and the gods.

Written in Akkadian, this story has reached us in two versions. The shorter one, from the middle of the second millennium, was probably written not long after it was composed; the other, written some thousand years later, is much longer and told in a different way. We have given it the name of its two heroes: *Nergal and Ereškigal.*[112]

The authors wanted to explain why and how the sovereignty of the netherworld, which mythological fantasy had organized as a state with its monarchs, functionaries, and capital palace, having long been ruled by a goddess, *Ereškigal* (in Sumerian: "Lady of the Great Territory," a name for the netherworld), was later brought under the rule of a god, *Nergal* (from the Sumerian *Nè-iri-gal*: "Authority of the Great City," another name for the same place), who had originally belonged to the larger group of "gods from on high."

The explanation is the same in both versions but is presented very differently. First, "each person is at home," Nergal on high, and Ereškigal below. The two meet and finally marry, and Nergal, in an unusual switch, joins his wife below in her infernal residence, instead of attracting her to his place on high. The earlier version portrays this union as the result of the brutal conquest of Ereškigal by Nergal, who is presented as a sort of dictator, whereas the long version turns the story into a true tale of boundless love: Nergal is seduced by Ereškigal, and Ereškigal by Nergal, and they end up, against all odds, never leaving each other again.

Here are the first lines of the short version, which gives the framework of the beginning of the story: the gods from on high are gathered together for a family meal, which they celebrate every month.[113]

> 1   When the gods prepared a banquet,
>   They sent a messenger
>   To their sister, Ereškigal,
>   "We cannot come down to you,
> 5   Nor can you come up to us.
>   Send (someone) here that they may take your food portion."
>   Ereškigal sent Namtar her messenger.
>   Up went N(amtar) to high heaven,
>   He entered (the place) the gods were (se)ated(?)
> 10 They interrupted their talk?, stood, recei(ved) Namtar,
>   The messenger of their great sister.

From this it appears that to share a meal, to participate in it, did not require one's physical presence. Appearing in person among the guests was not the important thing; what was, was "taking part in the festivities," in other words, eating the same thing as the other guests. A communion, not by one's presence but by the *food shared*.

So what was essential and sufficient was the nutritional as well as the enjoyment value of the food, which is, moreover, on reflection, quite logical: food was important, and valued, because it brought life, survival, to those who consumed it. That is what gave food its fundamental meaning, even if this notion is not explained, much less discussed, in any texts.

FOOD, LIFE, AND DEATH

Although to my knowledge the Mesopotamians never clearly explained themselves on this subject, they did not hide the importance they attributed to the maxim that *food brings life*. We have found echoes of this notion scattered through their writings, and it has been the guiding principle throughout the present work. It governed eating and drinking, cooking and the art of eating, and was hence a major component of thought and life in ancient Mesopotamia.

This is explained perhaps more explicitly in *The Adapa Story* (mentioned above), a fairly short tale in four or five fragments written in Akkadian (I believe an unpublished version existed in Sumerian).

Adapa (we don't know the real meaning of this word: it may have meant "wise man" in some language) was an *Apkallu*, something like an exceptional and legendary talent, one of the seven great civilizing heroes of the land,[114] and, as such, was linked closely to Ea, the inventor and great master of culture.

Despite Ea's interest in Adapa, we are immediately warned that

1   **To him (Ea) granted wisdom,**
    Eternal life he did not grant him,

following the logic of Ea's invention and creation of humans, who were distinguished from the gods mainly by their necessarily mortal destiny.

When Adapa went fishing one day in order to provide for the table of Ea in his temple at Eridu where Adapa was "cook," he was bothered by the south wind and broke off its wings. Following which he was summoned for an explanation by Anu, lord of the gods and of the world, who was irritated by the sudden paralysis of the wind, whose actions were indispensable for the economy of the land through the humidity and the rain that it provided.

Before Adapa appeared before Anu, Ea, his protector, whispered a warning to him about what awaited him and gave him some advice so that he would come out of it as best he could. Ea told Adapa that on his arrival at Anu's residence he would be presented with something to eat and drink, it being customary to offer a welcoming gift of that kind, but he should refuse it. For it would only be "good for the dead" and "drink for the dead," in other words, the food and drink reserved for mortals and made specifically to assure them life but also to ensure their mortality. On that occasion, however, Adapa could request the "food of life" and the "drink of life," which would render him immortal and similar to the gods. In refusing the first type of food and drink, he would no doubt be offered the second. As things turned out, Anu presented the second type to Adapa first:

60   "Bring him food of life, let him eat."
      They brought him food of life, he did not eat
      They brought him waters of life, he did not drink.

Upon which Anu began to laugh at the trick he thought he had played on Ea and his protégé, who thus, for having obeyed his master, lost his only chance to move into the ranks of the gods by becoming immortal.

Looking more closely, we see what the author subtly conveys, that the true winner in this padded duel was not Anu, contrary to appearances, but Ea, who had cleverly foreseen everything so that Adapa would remain mortal. Had he not from the start "assigned intelligence to him, wisdom," but "withheld endless life," so that he would always remain human?

The Adapa story, understood in this way, was one more piece to place into the thick file on the infallible glory of the most intelligent of gods.

But it unveils a new and profound idea by emphasizing the "food of life" and the "water of life," which opportunely develop the axiom above: not only does *"food give life,"* but it does so *proportionate to its nature.* According to the ancient Mesopotamians, foods did not, of course, include "murderers," which would immediately bring about death—that would be against the nature of food; but human food was mysteriously doctored (obviously by the gods) in such a way that it would provide its eaters with life, though a limited life; it would be incapable of preventing or interrupting death at the end of a given time, whereas the food and the water of life reserved only for the gods enabled the gods to live forever.

What we have here is an original mythological construction that explained the existence of immortal beings, on the one hand, and mortal ones, on the other. Even if the question seems never to have been formally developed as such, it must have been raised and must have inspired more than one explicative myth. This is one of them.

Life and death were thus found *in food.* To my knowledge, there has never been a further attempt to respond to the more basic question: Why and in what way did these two types of food differ in their consequences? But mythology never goes, and never can go, to the very heart of things. The ancient Mesopotamians were satisfied with this explanation alongside other answers: it was the will of the gods never to see humans rival them by equal immortality.

We can therefore call a halt to our investigation in the same spirit as we began it and carried it out: as curious students, not just about food in itself or how it was prepared, but primarily about the people who subsisted on it throughout so many centuries, who put it at the very center of their existence and their vision of things. Eating and drinking not only sustained them and kept them alive but enabled them to maintain their gods, and even their dead, with dignity, providing mortals with a response to the primal, dual question of why they lived and why they did not live forever.

CONCLUSION

In writing this book I did not intend to provide an exhaustive, scholarly study of eating and drinking among our venerable ancestors from ancient Mesopotamia. Such a work would have been tedious and dry, addressed (at the expense of honest readers) only to accademics, who scarcely need it and may not want it.

Nor did I have, even at the back of my mind, any intention of preparing a kind of cookbook of ancient Mesopotamian cuisine, the oldest known at present, "the oldest in the world." Such a project, for which we might naively hanker, must be abandoned once and for all, as it could never be written by a reasonable historian worthy of the name. Not only is our file much too narrow—fifty recipes at most—but it is inconceivable that anyone will ever boast of having filled with certainty the numerous gaps that have been left by thirty-five centuries of erosion. Nor will anyone ever be able to identify, from such a distance in time and space, the authentic flavor and quality of the scores of ingredients that were used in these culinary creations. We can never recover the taste, much less the true taste, of this rich and appetizing cuisine, whose refinement and brilliance we can only imagine.

Beginning from a more "anthropological" rather than strictly historical perspective, and taking advantage both of known texts and unexpected ones that have recently fallen into our hands, I have attempted to revive the image of the (at least) gastronomic pleasures of those ancient, inventive, intelligent, hard-working people who brought so much to humanity and who knew so well, when they could, how to appreciate the world around them. To recover, even in fragments, something of the authentic gastronomy created by the ancient Mesopotamians, perhaps the first people to engage in the art—might be a way to inspire in us as consumers, indeed as impenitent gourmets, through a kind of complicity, the "sympathy" (in the etymological sense of the word) indispensable for whoever wishes to truly know their fellow humans, those from the most distant past as well as those of today.

As for the immediate "pleasures of the table," since we are forced to abandon the hope of ever truly communing with the ancient Mesopotamians, might we not taste something like what they ate in the accomplishments of that "Turco-Arabic," "Lebanese," or "Middle Eastern" cuisine (however it is called) that is available to us? For this cuisine may well constitute a prolongation, a contemporary presentation, the only one available, of the lost Mesopotamian techniques of preparing and enjoying food and drink—the oldest cuisine in the world.

NOTES

1. In the slender columns of the *Küche* article, in vol. 6 of *RLA* (pp. 277–98). [See also J. Bottéro, "The Cuisine of Ancient Mesopotamia," pp. 36–47; and J. Bottéro, *Textes culinaires mésopotamiens.*—Trans.]

2. J. Bottéro, *Mesopotamia*, pp. 1ff.

3. *Deipnosophistai*, VII, 325.

4. Apicius, *De re coquinaria*.

5. There is, however, a very interesting work by Phyllis Pray Bober, *Art, Culture and Cuisine: Ancient and Medieval Gastronomy*, which discusses ancient cuisines, including those of prehistory and ancient Egypt.—Trans.

6. See note 1 above.

7. J. Bottéro and S. N. Kramer, *Lorsque les dieux . . .* , pp. 198ff.

8. *ARM XI*, no. 24.

9. *ARM XII*, no. 68.

10. *AbB I*, no. 106.

11. *AbB VI*, no. 22.

12. R. Labat, *Hémérologies*. Citation found on p. 50:8.

13. J. Bottéro, *Religion in Ancient Mesopotamia*, pp. 176ff.

14. See J. P. Vernant et al., *Divination et rationalité*, notably pp. 109–11; and "Oneiromancy," pp. 105–25, in J. Bottéro, *Mesopotamia*.

15. A. L. Oppenheim, *The Interpretation of Dreams*, pp. 270ff; 315ff. [The last three lines are not translated in Oppenheim, so I have translated from Bottéro's French text.—Trans.]

16. *MSL V*, p. 92.

17. E. Ebeling, *Tod und Leben*, pp. 9–19.

18. *ARM XI*, no. 13.

19. H. Hunger, *Kolophone*, no. 197:5, etc. The recipe may be found in R. P. Dougherty, *Archives from Erech*, no. 394.

20. B. Alster, *Instructions*, pp. 34ff.

21. English-language translations of all the recipes can be found in J. Bottéro, *Textes culinaires mésopotamiens*. Translations of selected recipes are in J. Bottéro, "The Cuisine of Ancient Mesopotamia." Rather than adopt those more scholarly translations in their entirety, however, I have chosen to borrow from them and to follow the author's format here as closely as possible in order to reflect his desire to appeal to a more general audience.—Trans.

22. W. G. Lambert, *Babylonian Wisdom Literature*, p. 215:13ff.

23. Kovacs, *The Epic of Gilgamesh*, pp. 8ff.

24. J. Bottéro, *L'Epopée de Gilgameš*, Philadelphia Tablet: 82ff, p. 223. [This citation is not in Kovacs's edition.—Trans.]

25. Kovacs, *The Epic of Gilgamesh*, pp. 15, 16.

26. Ibid., p. 16.

27. Ibid.

28. Ibid.

29. A. Leroi-Gourhan, *L'homme et la matière*, pp. 69ff.

30. Ibid., pp. 67ff.

31. Š/III, p. 297b.

32. J. Bottéro, *Religion in Ancient Mesopotamia*, pp. 114ff.

33. R. de Vaux, *Les institutions de l'Ancien Testament, II*, pp. 292ff.

34. *KAR*, 146, rev., right: 17.

35. Ibid., left obverse (22); right *20* and *23;* right reverse side: *13* and *14;* also F. Thureau-Dangin, *Rituels accadiens*, pp. 12ff: *6,* 14ff: *34;* 24ff: *5;* and again 124ff; *386.*

36. A. Maurizio, *Histoire de l'alimentation végétale*, p. 31.

37. W. Farber, *Beschwörungstrituale . . . .*, pp. 66:29ff.

38. F. Thureau-Dangin, *Rituels accadians*, pp. 12ff: *6;* 16ff:: *9,* etc.

39. A. Barrois, *Manuel d'archéologie biblique, I*, p. 322.

40. *CAD Q*, pp. 59ff.

41. M.-Th. Barrelet, "Dispositifs à feu et cuisson des aliments, à Ur, Nippur, Uruk," in *Paléorient* 3/2 (1974), pp. 243–300, followed on pp. 301–10 by an excellent tableau of contemporary data, by C. Bromberger.

42. A. Maurizio, *Histoire de l'alimentation végétale*, pp. 423ff.

43. J. Bottéro and S. N. Kramer, *Lorsque les dieux . . . ,* p. 684.

44. W. G. Lambert, *Babylonian Wisdom Literature*, p. 243, Rev. V:10ff.

45. A. Parrot, *Le Palais de Mari* (Mission archéologique de Mari II/3), *Documents et monuments* (Paris, 1959), pp. 33ff., and pl. XVI–XVII.

46. Ibid., p. 55.

47. A. Salonen, *Die Hausgeräte der alten Mesopotamier, II*, pp. 434ff.

48. "Onguent de pots," *ARM VII*, p. 173:3°.

49. *AbB II*, no. 89:31ff.

50. J. Bottéro and S. N. Kramer, *Lorsque les dieux . . . ,* p. 631.

51. L. Legrain, *Le temps des rois d'Ur*, no. 116:2.

52. *Ḫḫ* XVIII:128ff., *MSL VIII/2*, p. 120.

53. *Ḫḫ* XIII:93, *MSL VIII/2*, p.16.

54. G. Cros, *Nouvelles fouilles de Tellô*, pp. 81ff.

55. A. Salonen, *Die Fischerei*, pp. 273ff.

56. *CT XXII*, no. 221:5ff.

57. *SAA VIII*, no. 287.

58. Cig et al., *Die Puzris-Dagan Texte* p. 36, no. 102.

59. M. Schorr, *Altbabylonische Urkunden* (Leipzig, 1913), p. 335, no. 256.

60. Cited in *CAD M/II*, p. 162b.

61. *CAD M/I*, p. 286b.

62. J. André, *L'alimentation et la cuisine à Rome*, pp. 114, 198.

63. A. Salonen, *Die Fischerei*, p. 262.

64. *DP*, no. 331.

65. *HSS XIII*, no. 28:3.

66. M. Lambert and Ch. Virolleaud, *Textes économiques de Lagaš*, no. 46A; see also *Assyriological Studies*, 16, pp. 57ff; *The Philadelphia Onion Archive*, whose author, aghast at so much garlic, prefers to translate as "onion"!

67. A. Jaussen, *Coutumes des Arabes au pays de Moab*, 1907.

68. A. Maurizio, *Histoire de l'alimentation végétale*, p. 292.

69. A. Finet, *Le Code de Hammurapi* (Paris, 1973). For the reasons for the quotation marks around "code," see J. Bottéro, "The 'Code' of Hammurabi," *Mesopotamia*, pp. 156ff.

70. B. Alster, *The Instructions of Šuruppak*, p. 99:132.

71. J. van Dijk, *La sagesse numéro-accadienne*, p. 90.

72. M. Schorr, *Altbabylonische Urkunden*, no. 291S.

73. J. N. Strassmaier, *Cyrus*, no. 248, pp. 114ff.

74. *SAA VII*, no. 21; the text is in fragments.

75. *BaM XVI*, pp. 371ff.

76. English translation in Foster, *Before the Muses*, p. 430.—Trans.

77. *Epic of Gilgameš*, XI:83; J. Bottéro and S. N. Kramer, *Lorsque les dieux . . . ,* p. 571.

78. J. Bottéro, *Religion in Ancient Mesopotamia*, pp. 210-11.

79. Abydene version, J. Bottéro and S. N. Kramer, *Lorsque les dieux . . . ,* p. 577.

80. "Mouth" 𒅴 + "water" 𒀀 = "to drink" 𒅗 which through progressive stylization became 𒅗.

81. A. Boissier, *Documents assyriens . . . ,* p. 249, iv:9.

82. F. Thureau-Dangin, *Rituels accadiens*, pp. 75, 80.

83. M. Civil, *Studies Presented to A. Leo Oppenheim*, pp. 67-89. [Bottéro translates "liver" as "soul" (*âme*).—Trans.]

84. Regarding these divinities I refer the reader to the scholarly article by M. Krebernik in *RLA*, vol. 9, fasc. 5/6 (Berlin, 2000), pp. 442-44, s.v. *Nin-kasi und Siraš/Siris*.

85. B. Alster, *Proverbs of Ancient Sumer*, collection 2.123, vol. 1, p. 69.

86. *Ḫḫ XXIII, MSL XI*, pp. 69ff.

87. J. Cooper, *JCS XXVII*, pp. 163-74.

88. S. Maul has shown what motivated the fears of the innkeeper. The saloon was a place where sick people frequently went after a session with the exorcist. Among rituals he prescribed, the exorcist sometimes recommended that the patient, while talking quite naturally with other patrons, lightly touch the base of the fermenting vat, or the vat itself, while saying: "*Let Siris* (goddess of beer) *or Nigišzida* (god of the vine) *free me!*" Or perhaps the patient was to get rid of magi-

cally infected materials at the door of the saloon. "The business of the saloon," says the ritual, "will drop, but the evil will depart from the man and his house." These somewhat secondary infections motivated—in the most logical of ways for the ancient Mesopotamians—an exorcistic ritual which would cancel out their effects. *38e Rencontre assyriologique internationale* (Paris, 1992), pp. 389–96).

89. We can, however, note with interest the appearance of the logogram from the era called "Late Uruk" (before 3000) and above all the residue, quite probably of wine, in a pitcher from the same period (see V. R. Badler et al., *BaM XXVII* (1996), pp. 39–43.

90. E. Sollberger and J. R. Kupper, *Inscriptions royales,* p. 79.

91. *AbB* VI, no. 52:14ff.

92. *TCL,* XVIII, no. 133.

93. J. Bottéro and S. N. Kramer, *Lorsque les dieux . . . ,* pp. 115ff. [English translation from M. Civil, "Enlil and Ninlil: The Marriage of Sud," pp. 43–66.—Trans.]

94. Ibid., pp. 116–17. [Civil, p. 59.]

95. The author significantly employs the French word *vivres* for "food" in this paragraph, clearly showing its connection to "life," *vie,* "to live," *vivre* (cf. English "victuals" and "vitality"). Unfortunately, Bottéro's wordplay cannot be rendered in English.—Trans.

96. D. J. Wiseman, *Iraq XIV* (1952), 24–44.

97. *AfO XX* (1963), p. 38:34.

98. C. Günbatti, *Archivum Anatolicum* 3 (1997), p. 134.

99. Epilogue of the "Code" of Hammurabi, in A. Finet, *Le Code de Hammurapi* (1973), p. 136. [English translation in J. Bottéro, *Mesopotamia,* p. 168.—Trans.]

100. J. Bottéro and S. N. Kramer, *Lorsque les dieux . . . ,* pp. 602ff. [English translation of the myth in Foster, *Before the Muses;* the citations begin pp. 366ff.—Trans.]

101. Bottéro and Kramer, *Mythologie,* p. 619. [For "beer," on line 9, Foster writes "of the vine."—Trans.]

102. Ibid., p. 624.

103. Ibid., pp. 527ff.

104. Ibid., p. 641.

105. Translated and discussed in J. Bottéro and S. N. Kramer, *Lorsque les dieux . . . ,* pp. 527ff.

106. W. G. Lambert, *Babylonian Wisdom Literature,* p. 136:158.

107. E. Sollberger and J. R. Kupper, *Inscriptions royales,* p. 69:1G7ff.

108. Ibid., p. 170:140ff. [English translation in C. A. Benito, *"Enki and Ninmah"* and *"Enki and the World Order,"* p. 121.—Trans.]

109. English translations of the majority of the following excerpts may be found in J. Bottéro, *Religion in Ancient Mesopotamia,* p. 129.—Trans.

110. W. W. Hallo, "A Sumerian Amphictyony," *JCS,* XIV, pp. 88–116. [An English translation is not provided in Hallo's article; I have translated from the author's French version.—Trans.]

111. See J. J. Finkelstein, "The Genealogy of the Hammurapi Dynasty" *JCS* XX, pp. 95-118.

112. J. Bottéro and S. N. Kramer, *Lorsque les dieux* . . . , pp. 437ff. [English translation of citation in Foster, *Before the Muses*, pp. 414ff.—Trans.]

113. Ibid., pp. 438ff. [Foster, p. 414]

114. Ibid., pp. 93, 198ff. [English translations of cited passages in Foster, pp. 430, 433.—Trans.]

BIBLIOGRAPHY

Alster, B. *The Instructions of Suruppak*. Copenhagen, 1974.

———. *Proverbs of Ancient Sumer*. Bethesda, Md., 1997.

André, J. *L'alimentation et la cuisine à Rome*. Paris, 1961.

———. *Apicius. L'art culinaire [De re coquinaria]*. Paris, 1965.

Archivum Anatolicum. Ankara.

Assyriological Studies XVI: Studies in Honor of Benno Landsberger. Chicago, 1965.

Barrelet, M.-Th. *Dispositifs à feu et cuisson des aliments à Ur, Nippur, Uruk. Paléorient* 3/2, (1974), pp. 243–300.

Barrois, A. *Manuel d'archéologie biblique*. Paris, 1939.

Benito, C. A. *"Enki and Ninmah" and "Enki and the World Order"* (Microfilm). Ann Arbor, 1969.—Trans.

Bober, Phyllis Pray. *Art, Culture, and Cuisine: Ancient and Medieval Gastronomy*. Chicago, 1999.—Trans.

Boissier, A. *Documents assyriens relatifs aux présages*. Paris, 1894.

Bottéro, Jean. "The Cuisine of Ancient Mesopotamia." *Biblical Archaeologist*, March 1985:36–47.—Trans.

———. *L'Epopée de Gilgameš: Le grand homme qui ne voulait pas mourir*. Paris, 1992.

———. *Mésopotamie: L'écriture, la raison, et les dieux*. Paris, 1987. [English edition: *Mesopotamia: Writing, Reasoning, and the Gods*. Translated by Zainab Bahrani and Marc Van De Mieroop. Chicago, 1992.]

———. *La plus vieille religion: En Mésopotamie*. Paris, 1998. [English edition: *Religion in Ancient Mesopotamia*. Translated by Teresa Lavender Fagan. Chicago, 2001.]

———, *Textes culinaires mésopotamiens*, Winona Lake, Indiana, 1995.

Bottéro, J., and S. N. Kramer. *Lorsque les dieux faisaient l'homme: Mythologie mésopotamienne*. Paris, 1989.

Cig, M., H. Kizilay, and A. Salonen. *Die Puzriš-Dagan-Texte . . . , Teil I*. Helsinki, 1954.

Civil Miguel. "Enlil and Ninlil: The Marriage of Sud." *Journal of the American Oriental Society*, 103.11 (1983): 43–66.—Trans.

———. *Studies Presented to A. Leo Oppenheim*. Chicago, 1964.

Cros, G., *Nouvelles fouilles de Tellô*. Paris, 1910–14.

Deipnosophistai. Loeb Classical Library. *Atheneus, the Deipnosophists*, vol. 3. Cambridge, Mass., 1957.

De Vaux, R. *Les institutions de l'Ancien Testament*. Paris, 1960.

Dougherty, R. P. *Archives from Erech, Neo-Babylonian and Persian Period*. New Haven, 1933.

Ebeling, E. *Tod und Leben*. Berlin and Leipzig, 1931.

Farber, W. *Beschwörungsrituale an Ištar und Dumuzi*. Wiesbaden, 1977.

Finet, A. *Le Code de Hammurapi*. Paris, 1973.

Foster, Benjammin R. *Before the Muses: An Anthology of Akkadian Literature*, 2nd ed., 2 vols. Bethesda, Md., 1996. — Trans.

Herodotus. *The Persian Wars*. Translated by George Rawlinson, Introduction by F. R. B. Godolphin. New York, 1942. — Trans.

Hunger, H. *Kolophone: Babylonische und assyrische Kolophone*. Neukirchen-Vluyn, 1968.

Jaussen, A. *Coutumes des Arabes au pays de Moab*. Paris, 1908.

Kovacs, Maureen Gallery. *The Epic of Gilgamesh*. Stanford, Calif., 1985. — Trans.

Labat, R. *Hémérologies: Hémérologies et ménologies d'Assur*. Paris, 1939.

Lambert, M., and Ch. Virolleaud. *Tablettes économiques de Lagash*. Paris, 1968.

Lambert, W. G., *Babylonian Wisdom Literature*. Oxford, 1967.

Legrain, L. *Le temps des rois d'Ur*. Paris, 1912.

Leroi-Gourhan, A. *L'homme et la matière*. Paris, 1943.

Litke, R. L., *A Reconstruction of the Assyro-Babylonian God-lists. An:^{d}A-nu-um and An : Anu ša amēli*. New Haven, 1998.

Maurizio, A. *Histoire de l'alimentation végétale*. Paris, 1932.

Oppenheim, A. Leo, *The Interpretation of Dreams in the Ancient Near East*. Philadelphia, 1956.

Parrot, A. *Le Palais de Mari*. Paris, 1958 –.

Salonen, A. *Die Fischerei im alten Mesopotamien*. Helsinki, 1970.

———. *Die Hausgeräte der alten Mesopotamier*. Helsinki, 1965 –.

Schorr, M. *Altbabylonische Urkunden*. Leipzig, 1913.

Strabo. *The Geography of Strabo*. Loeb Classical Library, 7. Cambridge, Mass., 1961.

Strassmaier, J. N. *Inschriften von Cyrus, König von Babylon*. Leipzig, 1890.

Sollberger, E., and J. R. Kupper. *Inscriptions royales sumériennes et akkadiennes*. Paris, 1971.

Thureau-Dangin, F. *Rituels accadiens*. Paris, 1921.

Van Dijk, J. *La sagesse suméro-accadienne*. Leiden, 1953.

———. *Early Mesopotamian Incantations and Rituals*. New Haven, 1985. [vol. II of the Yale Oriental Series. Babylonian Texts]

Vernant, J.-P., et al. *Divination et rationalité*. Paris, 1974.